The Abingdon
Preaching
Annual

2018

Planning Sermons and Services
for Fifty-Two Sundays

Scott Hoezee, General Editor

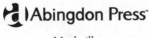

Abingdon Press™

Nashville

THE ABINGDON PREACHING ANNUAL 2018:
PLANNING SERMONS AND SERVICES FOR FIFTY-TWO SUNDAYS

Copyright © 2017 by Abingdon Press

All rights reserved.

This book is printed on acid-free paper.

Library of Congress Cataloging-in-Publication Data has been requested.

ISBN 978-1-5018-3553-7

17 18 19 20 21 22 23 24 25 26—10 9 8 7 6 5 4 3 2 1
MANUFACTURED IN THE UNITED STATES OF AMERICA

Contents

🌿 = Sunday in Lent   ✹ = Sunday of Advent

ESSAYS FOR SKILL-BUILDING

FULL SERMON TEXTS

Acknowledgments

Publishing a book is always a collaborative enterprise, and never more so than when it's a collection of the work of many writers. For this 2018 preaching annual I am incredibly grateful to every person who agreed to write up a batch of sermon starters and for all those who also submitted sample sermons to be published. I am grateful for their creativity and the generous spirit with which they went about their task of coming up with these homiletical and liturgical ideas. Here and there along the way I made a couple of mistakes or was guilty of less-than-clear communication, but I am thankful for the grace these writers showed at those times too.

Constance Stella and Peggy Shearon of Abingdon / The United Methodist Publishing House were there every step along the way, too, as were the good people who sent out contracts, looked up copyrights, did page designs, and made sure that all things were done in good order. I am also grateful to my Center for Excellence in Preaching colleague, Mary Bardolph, who in both the 2017 volume and now this year's volume helped to make the formatting consistent and developed the book's indices. Every day I am happy to work with Mary, and that includes this project as well.

—Scott Hoezee, General Editor

Editor's Introduction

The rock singer Sting has a song called "Seven Days." The lyrics are really about his hesitant, up-and-down resolve to get in touch with a woman he's interested in. But I have long thought the song applies equally well to pastors as they ponder the weekly task of sermon writing and just when it is you should get rolling on it. The song's refrain begins "Monday, I could wait till Tuesday" and then proceeds through the rest of the week until finally he's running out of days and concludes "Saturday could wait. *But Sunday'd be too late...*"

Yes, Sunday would be too late to crank up the vital task of coming up with a new sermon. But since I run a sermon-idea website at Calvin Theological Seminary's "Center for Excellence in Preaching," I can assure you that every single week Saturday sees the highest traffic on the website (and Sunday is not exactly a quiet day on the site either)!

The volume you are holding is our effort for the 2018 calendar year to make that job of sermon preparation at least a little easier. In this volume you will find energizing ideas and insights from some fellow preachers with the hope that something will spark a novel way to view a given text or present just enough of a new slant on a familiar text as to make that text seem new after all.

We have also provided some sample litanies, prayers, and other liturgical resources to make the weekly task of cobbling together worship services a bit easier even as these resources also go along with the preaching themes presented on lectionary texts. The hope is that something in these pages will provide the needed jolt of creativity every preacher longs for. Writing sturdy, true, and fresh sermons is the preacher's number one task every week. It takes a lot of time to do it and, remember, Sunday would be too late. But blessings to you, my fellow preachers, as you engage this ongoing holy work for God's people.

—*Scott Hoezee, General Editor*

January 6, 2018—Epiphany

Passages: Isaiah 60:1-6; Psalm 72:1-7, 10-14; Ephesians 3:1-12; Matthew 2:1-12

Gathering Prayer

Holy and living God, thank you for your faithfulness and steadfast love since the moment you created the universe. Thank you for the many ways you draw all of creation closer to you. Reveal to us how we might serve you, love you, and truly be your hands and feet in our world. You are alive and active each and every day. Awaken my senses, quicken my heart, and lead me to speak and act in tune with your rhythm for your creation.

Preaching Theme

Ephesians 3:1-12 reveals the great epiphany that the gospel was always meant to be for both those of Jewish descent and non-Jewish descent (Gentiles) alike.

Throughout the New Testament, we find multiple references to Peter and Paul debating what it means to be a disciple of Jesus. Can you imagine what *that* was like for the early Christian churches at this time? Comparing the résumés of Paul and Peter was an exercise in comparing polar opposites. Peter was one of Jesus's closest friends and confidants, yet he also denied him when things were blackest. Paul was outspoken about his storied history of viciously attacking early Christians, yet everything changed with his dramatic meeting with Jesus on the road to Damascus (Acts 9). How did the followers of The Way know whom to believe and how to live as faithful disciples?

In the Common English Bible translation of this passage in Ephesians, the Apostle Paul shares God's *secret plan* about Jesus the Christ. Another way of translating the words *secret plan* is *mystery*. In these action-packed verses, Paul reveals an epiphany, an *a-ha* moment, that would change the trajectory of the good news of Jesus for all of humanity.

What controversies and debates within the church, in either our history or present day, remind you of Paul's letter to the house church in Ephesus? How does our history as a church that relies on the continual revelation of the Holy Spirit, guide your preaching today? Does diversity mean that we must think and act exactly alike?

Secondary Preaching Themes

Matthew 2:1-12

Imagine the expectation that the mysterious wise men from the east had. What do their gifts of gold, frankincense, and myrrh reveal about their hopes and dreams for the Messiah? How are their hopes and expectations different than Herod's response?

Isaiah 60:1-6

The gift of hope shifts from earlier parts of Isaiah. The focus moves to the gift of community. How does the revelation of epiphany provide salvation to the community that is facing restoration from exile from the Third Prophet Isaiah?

Responsive Reading (based on Psalm 72:1-7)

God, give your judgments to the king.

Give your righteousness to the king's son.

Let him judge your people with righteousness and your poor ones with justice.

Let the mountains bring peace to the people; let the hills bring righteousness.

Let the king bring justice to people who are poor; let him save the children of those who are needy, but let him crush oppressors!

Let the king live as long as the sun, as long as the moon, from generation to generation.

Let him fall like rain upon fresh-cut grass, like showers that water the earth.

Let the righteous flourish throughout their lives, and let peace prosper until the moon is no more.

Responsive Reading (based on Psalm 72:10-15)

Let the kings of Tarshish and the islands bring tribute; let the kings of Sheba and Seba present gifts.

Let all the kings bow down before him; let all the nations serve him.

Let it be so, because he delivers the needy who cry out, the poor, and those who have no helper.

He has compassion on the weak and the needy; he saves the lives of those who are in need.

He redeems their lives from oppression and violence; their blood is precious in his eyes.

Let the king live long! Let Sheba's gold be given to him!

Let him be prayed for always! Let him be blessed all day long!

Repentance Prayer

Forgive us for the many moments that we choose comfort over speaking against what is popular. Forgive us for the times when we let our need to be right supersede your prophetic calling for us. Help us to take ownership of the prayer you taught us, when we pray for your will to be done in this kingdom and the next.

Benediction

May the God of peace be with you today. May we calibrate our senses to become more aware of the Sacred One who moves in and through all of creation today. May we seek sacred a-ha moments each day as God continually reveals God's self to us.

January 7, 2018

Passages: Genesis 1:1-5; Psalm 29; Acts 19:1-7; Mark 1:4-11

Gathering Prayer (inspired from Genesis 1:1-5)

Creator of all that is, all that was, and all that ever will be, you are light, and you separated light from darkness. You created the heavens and the earth. You gave shape and form to the sea and the land. You breathed life into everything that moves above, on, or beneath it. Come to us now in this moment and time. Remind us of what an incredible gift it is to sit in your presence, Creating, Redeeming, and Sustaining One. As we open ourselves to studying your holy scriptures, reveal yourself to us in a new and powerful way. Come, Holy Spirit, come.

Preaching Theme

Remember, repent, and renew. In the Gospel of Mark, John the Baptist reminds everyone who would hear him that God's love is constant throughout time. John tells the people that the Lord who saved when they were still slaves in Egypt is still the God who is moving and acting today. If repentance means to turn away from their sins, then the wilderness may be the perfect place to call people to a deeper, more honest, more elemental relationship with God. John's life, clothing, and actions were consistent with someone purely focused on calling God's people to such a renewed relationship with God's self. While John's fame and influence grows, it seems that his laser focus on the Messiah to come never wavers. By the time we get to verses 9-11, John's cousin Jesus arrives just in time to be baptized himself.

What are some of the ways that this passage in Mark 1 helps us as modern-day prophets who are called to point to the life of Christ? What does it mean to lead the flocks we are called to serve in a way that prepares *our* people for the coming of Christ again? How do our lives and particularly this sermon draw attention away from our own words and to the ultimate gift of love in Jesus?

Just after Mark 1:11, Jesus is *forced* into the wilderness, where he would be tempted for forty days. How might we prepare our people not just for the mountain-top experiences of baptism but also for the temptations that lie before us?

Secondary Preaching Themes (Acts 19:1-7)

In John 14:26, we read about the promise Jesus makes to his followers that a *Companion* (or in some translations, *Advocate)* will be revealed. The Holy Spirit was promised to teach us and remind us of everything that Jesus had said and done. This passage is helpful in interpreting Acts 19. In these first seven verses, we read about believers in Ephesus who had been taught, initially, by Apollos. But Apollos never shared about the Holy Spirit because he didn't know about the Holy Spirit. When Paul baptized these disciples in Ephesus, the Holy Spirit began working in them in wondrous and miraculous ways.

Responsive Reading (based on Psalm 29)

You, divine beings! Give to the Lord—give to the Lord glory and power!

Give to the Lord the glory due his name!

Bow down to the Lord in holy splendor!

The Lord's voice is over the waters; the glorious God thunders; the Lord is over the mighty waters.

The Lord's voice is strong; the Lord's voice is majestic.

The Lord's voice breaks cedar trees—yes, the Lord shatters the cedars of Lebanon.

He makes Lebanon jump around like a young bull, makes Sirion jump around like a young wild ox.

The Lord's voice unleashes fiery flames; the Lord's voice shakes the wilderness—yes, the Lord shakes the wilderness of Kadesh.

The Lord's voice convulses the oaks, strips the forests bare,

but in his temple everyone shouts, "Glory!"

The Lord sits enthroned over the floodwaters; the Lord sits enthroned—king forever!

Let the Lord give strength to his people! Let the Lord bless his people with peace!

Benediction

May the breadth and depth of the Holy Spirit descend upon us as we seek to be followers of Jesus Christ. May the Holy Spirit teach us to think, to learn, to grow, and to respond to God's grace in such a way that all those around us may experience the incredible grace of our Lord and Savior Jesus Christ today. May we glow in God's grace, so that the grace of the Spirit may grow in each and every one of us. Go now in the peace and understanding that we worship God who is active and alive today.

January 14, 2018

Passages: *1 Samuel 3:1-10 (11-20); Psalm 139:1-6, 13-18; 1 Corinthians 6:12-20; John 1:43-51*

Gathering Prayer

Lord Jesus, reveal yourself to us this day. Make our hearts, minds, and very beings sensitive to your life-saving activity. Just as your prophets Samuel and Eli waited daily for you, instill in us the ability to wait patiently for you, God, above all else.

Preaching Theme

"A Flickering Light of Hope"—This week's primary theme is a focus on waiting with anticipation for the word of the Lord in the ordinary days of our lives.

In 1 Samuel 3, we learn that getting a direct word from the Lord was rare in Samuel's day. In the very first verse, the author tells us that visions weren't widely known. We know now that soon after this passage was written, the Israelites would experience a transformation in Israel...but first they needed to hear God's word.

Here is Samuel, a child who has been serving God and learning from the teachings of his mentor, Eli. Eli and his family have already been warned multiple times before this passage that they have abused their priestly authority and their time of pastoral care was coming to an end. But, Samuel is still serving under Eli, and the word of the Lord is very rare those days, visions were rare...the people wanted to hear God, but they somehow couldn't.

How poetic is it that Eli, once a great prophet, lost his way and began to lose his sight. Even the light of God is waning in the temple, but the light is not out! God speaks to a child and we learn that even in this time of prophetic stillness, God's word and promises will come to fruition.

Guided Meditation

When we ask, "Where is God?" are we really expecting a response? We come to you, O God, seeking to encounter you this day...

Maybe we forgot how to listen to God's word…

Teach us, Lord, to listen for your word today…

Maybe we doubt that God still talks today…

Form us, Lord, to sit in our doubts so that our faith may be in you…

Maybe we are not willing to listen, because we don't know if we can follow through if we do hear from you…

Maybe, just maybe… we don't know where to begin.

Thank you, loving and living God, that while there are moments when we don't know how to begin, you sit with us exactly where we are and your grace compels us to grow in your image.

Secondary Preaching Themes

1 Corinthians 6:12-20

In this scripture passage, the focus is on sexual immorality. In what ways do our bodies provide an act of worship rather than draw us away from God? How do our intimate relationships call us into a deeper focus on the author and perfecter of our faith?

John 1:43-51

Here we find that Jesus called two ordinary people, Philip and Nathanael, into ministry. We remember that it was Philip (in John 6) who asked if there was enough food to go around for five thousand to be fed. It was Nathanael (in John 1) whose hometown had such a bad reputation that folks wondered if anything good could ever come from there.

Responsive Reading (based on Psalm 139:1-6)

Lord, you have examined me.

You know me.

You know when I sit down and when I stand up.

Even from far away, you comprehend my plans.

You study my traveling and resting.

You are thoroughly familiar with all my ways.

There isn't a word on my tongue, Lord, that you don't already know completely.

You surround me—front and back.

You put your hand on me.

That kind of knowledge is too much for me;

it's so high above me that I can't fathom it.

Responsive Reading (based on Psalm 139:13-18)

You are the one who created my innermost parts;

you knit me together while I was still in my mother's womb.

I give thanks to you that I was marvelously set apart.

Your works are wonderful—I know that very well.

My bones weren't hidden from you

when I was being put together in a secret place,

when I was being woven together in the deep parts of the earth.

Your eyes saw my embryo, and on your scroll every day was written that was being formed for me,

before any one of them had yet happened.**God, your plans are incomprehensible to me!**

Their total number is countless! If I tried to count them—they outnumber grains of sand!

If I came to the very end—I'd still be with you.

Benediction

May the awesome gift of God be with you this day. May you wait patiently and anticipate with urgency the calling of God. As you do, may you be blessed.

January 21, 2018

Passages: Jonah 3:1-5, 10; Psalm 62:5-12; 1 Corinthians 7:29-31; Mark 1:14-20

Gathering Prayer

God, you are the one who calls us to be ministers of your gospel. We lay our fishing nets, gifts, talents, professions, and even our shortcomings at your feet as an act of worship. We want to follow you, but we confess that too often we speak when we should listen. Too often we sit by when you call us to act, and far too often we weigh the cost of discipleship and choose the easy, lightweight, couch-potato option. Do with us what you will. Shape us as you desire and make us into the disciples you are calling us to be. May this be your day, for it always was.

Preaching Theme

Responding when it matters most—the primary theme for this week is the incredible responses from Simon, Peter, James, and John (maybe the Ninevites too).

In Mark 1:14-20, Jesus's ministry begins right after his cousin, John the Baptist, is sent to prison. We don't know why John's imprisonment launched this stage of formal ministry for Jesus. Similar to the prophet Jonah who tells the people of Nineveh to repent, Jesus's call for repentance is efficient with few words. But while Jesus's word count is low, the impact of his words is incredible.

In the Common English Bible translation, Jesus says, "Now is the time! Here comes God's kingdom! Change your hearts and lives, and trust this good news!" While preaching this poignant and proficient sermon, Jesus calls Simon and Andrew along with the sons of Zebedee away from their fishing profession.

Take a step back and consider the magnitude of these four men's decision. It's extremely likely that these fishermen inherited their vocational trade from their fathers, who likely learned from their fathers. We don't know exactly how many generations of fishermen these men had followed. We do know that once they encountered Jesus, they left the security of their jobs to follow him. More than security, they likely faced initial scrutiny from their friends and families for following a little-known prophet named Jesus. Maybe that's why, toward the end of the Gospel of John, so many of the disciples returned to fishing after Jesus rose from the dead. These men grew up on the sea. How is it possible that Jesus could have pulled them away from the one thing they knew so well? Had they been waiting for an opportunity to go into ministry?

How does the good news of the gospel call us to lay everything aside for the sake of the kingdom of Jesus? What does it mean to be followers of Jesus in the way that Simon, Andrew, James, and John were? How might we calibrate or completely shift away from our comforts and the things we know best to share a gospel that is so urgently needed?

Secondary Preaching Themes

1 Corinthians 7:29-31

In these verses, we find some examples of living and being that at first may seem contradictory. Reflect on the ways that having a kingdom perspective in this world opens up our perspective. What does it mean to be aware of the here and now while staying focused on the return of the Messiah?

Jonah 3:1-5, 10

Here we find one of the shortest repentance sermons in the entire Bible. The reluctant prophet Jonah walks through a town for roughly three days and recites, "Just forty days more and Nineveh will be overthrown!" Nine words changed the trajectory of Nineveh forever. How does Jonah's story and the story of Nineveh apply to our world today from a preaching context?

Responsive Reading (based on Psalm 62:5-8)

Oh, I must find rest in God only,

because my hope comes from him!

Only God is my rock and my salvation—

my stronghold!—I will not be shaken.

My deliverance and glory depend on God.

God is my strong rock. My refuge is in God.

All you people: Trust in him at all times!

Pour out your hearts before him!

God is our refuge!

Responsive Reading (based on Psalm 62:9-12)

Human beings are nothing but a breath.

Human beings are nothing but lies.

They don't even register on a scale;

taken all together they are lighter than a breath!

Don't trust in violence;

don't set false hopes in robbery.

When wealth bears fruit,

don't set your heart on it.

God has spoken one thing—make it two things—that I myself have heard:

that strength belongs to God,

and faithful love comes from you, my Lord—

and that you will repay

everyone according to their deeds.

Benediction

May the God who called Simon, Andrew, James, and John call your name today. May you hear God's calling through the whisper of a gentle breeze or as clear as your name as the cheer of a crowd. As you seek to follow Jesus, may you be blessed.

January 28, 2018

Passages: *Deuteronomy 18:15-20; Psalm 111; 1 Corinthians 8:1-13; Mark 1:21-28*

Gathering Prayer

Almighty God, you calm the raging waters and you speak peace to the troubled soul. Send your Spirit to dwell among us that we might hear your word over the chaos. Give us ears to hear that which gives life. Transform us in the way of Christ, that your love may be made known through us, in our time and in this place. In your name we pray, Amen.

Preaching Theme

Mark's Gospel is not known for wordiness or narrative excess. I always say that John's is the English major's Gospel. The sit-down-and-stay-awhile storytelling with vivid imagery and poetic phrasing. Mark's is just the opposite. Mark's is the Twitter Gospel. The story told in as few characters as possible, with little embellishment. The result is an abiding sense of urgency: Let's go. We've got work to do. I'll explain later.

Which is how Jesus engages the unclean spirit in this episode. Succinctly, authoritatively, and with zero drama. "Be gone with you," he says, as one who has the authority to command such things. Which, of course, he does. This is the central lesson of the story, and one of the key messages of Mark's Gospel: Jesus holds power over all elements, human and otherwise, worldly and otherworldly. He does not have time to mess around, over-explaining his every move. Follow him now and figure out the details later. Even the spirits obey him...

This notion of "possession" is so foreign to our contemporary context that many preachers are tempted to substitute the unclean spirit with a modern-day mental illness. A cautionary word in that regard: exploring mental illness as a sort of otherworldly influence can be dangerous territory. Even with the best of intentions, such interpretation can be fraught with all sorts of unintended implications for the hearer. A better approach—and a more textually accurate one—would be to explore modern-day understandings of authority. What people or institutions influence our daily decisions, for better or worse? Where do we get our news? What sources do we trust, and why? Whose opinions matter to us? And what impact do all of these voices have on our faith life?

Enter into that crowded circle of influence: Jesus. What does he have to say in the daily barrage of messages that we encounter? How might his words transform the other voices we have to process, and what "unclean spirits" might we need to exorcise in order to fully embody his spirit of love and mercy?

Secondary Preaching Themes (1 Corinthians 8:1-13)

A text about food law that is not really about food law. Or rather, does not have to be about food law, for a contemporary audience. The gist is that the community of faith is no longer bound by some of the ancient code that distinguished them as God's people. God has deemed "clean" for them much of what was forbidden. However, Paul cautions that even the *appearance* of breaking the law can damage public relations. Is eating this newly allowed meat worth it, in the grand scheme of things, if it causes them to seem hypocritical? This is just one of many instances that demonstrates Paul's gift for understanding context, and shaping the message of the gospel for a particular time and place. This passage is not necessarily about whether or not to eat meat but more about the importance of discernment when it comes to adherence to the law. What do we follow and why? The question provides an opportunity for the modern-day faith community to explore its own messaging: What signs, symbols, or verbal cues do we employ, and what message do they convey to the community around us? In what ways do we hold on to ancient laws that no longer serve us? What do we follow and why?

The movie *Footloose* comes to mind: a town devoid of joy because of one faith leader's attachment to an archaic notion of purity. That narrative was transformed by the youthful energy of the lead characters, and the story ends with dancing. Lots of dancing. The message is not "progress for the sake of progress." But rather, a challenge to explore deeply what we value and why.

Offering Meditation

Today a picture in a magazine will tell you that your look is not right—try this new wardrobe, or this new hair product. A radio ad will tell you that you need a new car. A TV commercial will insist that you must have a new cell phone. The Open House sign on your corner might beckon, "This way to your dream home."

You will hear hundreds of these messages today. And every day. They are all invitations to spend yourself. Not just your money, but your very self, in the pursuit of things that will not give you life.

The invitation to constant, unfettered acquisition is an "unclean spirit" in the life of our faith and culture. Those messages keep us isolated and anxious and fill us with a constant sense of inadequacy. Sharing some of your gifts with the church is a way of casting out that spirit of scarcity; a way of saying that those other voices do not have authority in your life. This is how we begin to place our trust in the redemptive presence of Christ in the world. Let us give joyfully to the one who makes us whole.

February 4, 2018

*Passages: Isaiah 40:21-31; Psalm 147:1-11, 20c; 1 Corinthians 9:16-23;
Mark 1:29-39*

Call to Worship (Psalm 147)

Leader: Praise the Lord! How good it is to sing praises to our God

People: God is gracious: a song of praise is fitting!

Leader: The Lord builds up the fallen; the Lord gathers the outcast.

People: God heals the brokenhearted and binds up their wounds.

Leader: God determines the number of the stars

People: And gives to all of them their names.

Leader: Great is our Lord, and abundant in power

People: Sing to the Lord with thanksgiving!

Leader: Praise the one who covers the heavens with clouds, prepares rain for the
earth, makes grass grow on the hills.

People: The one who gives to the animals their food

Leader: God's delight is not in the strength of the horse, nor in the speed of a
runner.

**People: The Lord takes pleasure in those who worship, who hope in God's
steadfast love.**

Preaching Theme

If this passage played out on the big screen, it would be a montage: a series of
brief images, in rapid succession, that imply the passage of time and the progress
of the narrative. After healing Simon's mother-in-law, Jesus heals a large gathering
of folks from a wide range of maladies. Although these other people may not have
names and faces, the sheer volume of those healed in quick succession bears the

far-reaching implications of Jesus's ministry. In the fast-paced rhythm of Mark's Gospel, we are led to assume that what happened here, happened in many places. Thus, the montage effect. In the span of thirty seconds, we glimpse the bigger picture of what life was about in those days.

Notice, then, the importance of the "quiet place," where Jesus takes himself to pray. That Sabbath moment appears as a stark contrast in what is otherwise a flurry of activity. The eye at the heart of a frenzied storm. And, of course, they come looking for him.

"Everyone is searching for you." Well, wouldn't they be? After they've seen what can be done in his presence?

Renewed in prayer, Jesus gets up and goes to the next place. There will be more teaching, more preaching, more healing of the masses. Perhaps he is ready—renewed in the spirit by his brief time of silence.

While the sermon could certainly focus on the healing of Simon's mother-in-law—and the way in which she went about her work after being made well—this could also be a valuable opportunity for the church to examine its mission-focus practices. Are we rushing through a packed program year, trying to be all things to all people, engaging in a flurry of high-energy activity, without pausing to fully renew ourselves in worship and prayer? If so, how can we realign and reimagine our shared ministry in ways that more faithfully mirror the Jesus kind of rhythm—seeking a stillness in the heart of all the movement, where we can be made new for the journey ahead.

Turn on the news and see if you can find an up-to-the minute story of peaceful protest: people showing up for racial justice, an end to hunger, or a ceasefire. Any place where people are standing still and silent in the midst of chaos. What can we learn from those modern-day images, and similar figures throughout history, about how to be a prayerful presence in the midst of great movement and change?

Secondary Preaching Themes (Isaiah 40:21-31)

"Mount up with wings like eagles." That's one of those scriptural turns-of-phrase that has been committed to our musical lexicon in more arrangements than we can count.

Following the Babylonian exile, the people of God had an all-too-clear understanding of the transient nature of human life. They scarcely need Isaiah, their prophet-in-residence, to remind them that "the grass withers, and the flower fades..." They had lived with withering and fading for years! They know, in their weary bones, that even a return from wilderness does not mean immortality.

But that communal awareness of finitude renders the poetry all the more powerful: all is not lost. God still holds power over all the oppressive powers of earth, and even transcends the body's weakness in age. Even the oldest and most frail among them will be given flight. This passage, often read in the funeral service, also has its Sunday morning potential: in our human smallness, the grandeur of God is made known.

If we need to see how this works in real time, maybe a field trip to a national park is in order. Or at the very least a guided meditation. At the foot of the Rocky Mountains, at the edge of the Grand Canyon, or in some small chasm of Zion, we glimpse that thin place where we end and the next holy thing begins.

Benediction

May God be known in the stillness; may the holy be found in our smallness; and may Christ be made known in our ordinary rhythms of love and grace. Amen.

What Am I Doing Here?

Mark 1:29-39

Karoline M. Lewis

My son plays hockey. I do not like hockey, I really, really don't. Now, I realize that at this point, as a preacher, I may not be "reading my context" very well. I live and work in Minnesota, after all, and I fully expect that many of you have now written me off, perhaps forever. "I can't possibly take preaching with her! What kind of Minnesotan is she? Not a hockey fan? Is there even room for her in heaven?" I get it.

I just think that if it takes forty-five minutes to put stuff on your body to protect yourself from serious injury, well, maybe that's something you should not be doing in the first place. Also, being in the warming room, the locker room, whatever you want to call it, helping my son get on the gear and lace up the skates, here's the thing: there's simply not enough deodorant *in the world* to make that smell go away.

What am I doing here? I don't like hockey. I'm freezing my you-know-what off even in an indoor ice rink and not even my venti nonfat no-foam latte from Starbucks can help.

But this past week, there I was. My ten-year-old son's first playoff game, swearing I would *never* do this, but screaming with the rest of parents, "Get in there! Go for the puck!" like my son could even hear me. And here's the weird thing. I was actually *watching* the game. I had been to many games, but they were outside, and I was in and out of my car trying to thaw myself out, spending most of the time in denial that my youngest son was even playing hockey in the first place. But, at this playoff game, I realized, wow, this is a really hard sport. This takes a lot of skill. It's a fight for the puck at every turn. And, they won! They beat an undefeated team and moved forward to the next playoff game. For all intents and purposes, this is exciting! Yet, at the same time, I'm watching my son's head hit the ice, a lot of very sharp skates coming dangerously close to his face, and wondering if the gear that took forty-five minutes to put on will really protect him, because it didn't for Jack Jablonski.

What am I doing here?

Maybe this was the question Simon's mother-in-law asked when she first realized she was healed.

The healing of Simon's mother-in-law is a *classic* healing story. It's all fine and good. It's what Jesus does. It's what he's good at. But there is something sort of disturbing about this story that doesn't seem to have anything to do with healing. "The fever left her, and she served them." What? She's healed so that she can serve? Whom? Did she want to? That's all she could do? Didn't she have any other aspirations? If you are brought back from the edge, from almost death, or from the brink of what you thought your life had to be, shouldn't there be something else for you, some sort of new vocation, new career, new identity? And she served them? As if that was what she was *expected* to do. As if that was the only thing she *thought* she could do. As if that was the *only thing* she could do?

But, what if the healing of Simon's mother-in-law was bringing her back to be the mother she always was and that she always wanted to be? And in being brought back to *who* she was, she became a disciple, called to minister, to serve, like the angels did for Jesus in the wilderness and like the Son of Man, who did not come to be served but to serve?

Have you ever felt like God has brought you back from the brink...to yourself? That you were called back from a place that was not fully you, to be you?

Jesus lifted her up. What if resurrection is being raised up to be who you always were and were always meant to be? That it won't be hilltop houses, driving fifteen cars, or bathrooms you can play baseball in, but the radical, emotional, incredible feeling of being you. That being raised up is not just some sort of spiritual future but your present reality, here and now, to live *you*. Your mind, spirit, body, everything together, everything that you were always meant to be. The story of Simon's mother-in-law tells us that God does not call us to be something we are not but is in the business of restoring us to who we really are.

Of course, most of the time it's easier to live on the brink, to surround yourself with people and projects and performances that allow you to pretend this is you, that let you avoid the feelings and frustrations and fears that come with acknowledging what is important in your life. It is *so* hard to live who you are. To paraphrase one of my favorite quotes, "The world is full of people who will go their whole lives and not actually live one day. I do not intend on being one of them." And, as one of my dear friends says often, "So much keeps us from living from the center of our being."

I think a lot of us spend a good part of our lives living on the periphery of ourselves.

So, on this past Saturday, at that playoff game, in an ice-cold ice rink, God took my hand and lifted me up. Bringing me back from the brink of tenure review and meetings and book proposals and syllabi writing and curricular revision and grading and course scheduling. Which is a lot of me but not all of me. Raising me up to be me because being a mom is not, "I'm just a mom." And serving is not just service.

The healing of Simon's mother-in-law, *and I so wish she had a name*, is *God being, living who God is*. God called Jesus to be who he was. That's what the incarnation is all about. Jesus didn't go around pretending to be something that he wasn't. "Please, please, let this cup pass. My God, my God, why have you forsaken *me?*" Are not laments about what *should* be but the truth about what is? Being human is to what God committed Godself and therefore, being who we are is what God wants us to be. God brings us back from the brinks of our lives, from despair, from disease, from desperation, to live. Because then, maybe, we will actually know, feel, and get that *we* are a part, that God needs us to be a part, of what's at stake for God when God decided to become one of us.

I am reminded of a sermon preached by one of our recent graduates, *on this text*, after having been diagnosed with breast cancer weeks into her first call. Now cancer free, she's been brought back from the brink. Jesus took her by the hand. God raised her up. When you are brought back from the edge, your question is, "What am I doing here?" Her answer? "I am a preacher. That's who God wants me to be. This is who I am." And now, at least in my mind, Simon's mother-in-law has a name. And now, it may even be mine.

February 11, 2018– Transfiguration Sunday

Passages: 2 Kings 2:1-12; Psalm 50:1-6; 2 Corinthians 4:3-6; Mark 9:2-9

Gathering

God of the mountaintop, be known to us in this place. Send your Spirit to move among us, that we might glimpse your glory in all that lies around us. Open our eyes to the wonder of this day, this hour, this moment. Let us dwell for a time in your presence, that we might be renewed for the journey ahead. Speak your calling on our lives again and make us one in the hope that we find in you. In your name we pray, Amen.

Preaching Theme

We've all been there...the mountaintop where, for the briefest of moments, all seems right with the world. We have "arrived," and we want to rest. We want to set up camp and stay there forever. So we can certainly sympathize with Peter when, having arrived at this critical moment with Jesus, he wants to put some stakes in the ground. He asks to build three dwellings—one for Jesus, one for Moses, one for Elijah—so that they can all stay there, happily ensconced on that mountain, forever.

"Nope," says Jesus. "We still go on."

As is typical in Mark's Gospel, there is always some next thing to be getting on with.

What Peter has been able to glimpse here is some fullness of time; some thin and holy scenario where these three critical moments in the Hebraic narrative are drawn into a single place in time. Perhaps he also glimpsed there the way that Jesus would soon join the company of these other two prophets, gone on to God and present only in memory. The power of that must have been as heartbreaking as it was dazzling. Of course he wanted to stay there forever and keep Jesus in the safety of some mountaintop haven.

But, of course, they couldn't stay. No perfect moment can stay. So for preaching today, maybe we can all explore a few of our own mountaintop moments: the last night of church camp, the answered prayer, the return from some long wilderness, the healing of some broken connection....In those places we glimpse some holy fulfillment of all God's promises, all of our hopes, and all the mystery of creation. It is natural to want to put up a flag and stay there forever. But since we can't—what truth can we take from the mountaintop that will sustain us for the journey ahead?

Secondary Preaching Themes (2 Kings 2:1-12)

"Elisha went over." So much narrative potential in those three little words. In addition to setting the stage as a prequel to the transfiguration story, this episode could stand all on its own as a sermon about transitions. Or, more specifically, a sermon about leadership and legacy.

If the transfiguration leads us to examine what we take with us from the mountaintop, then perhaps this one might engage us in questions about what we leave for those who come after?

In what ways do we equip the next generation of leaders to "carry the mantle" of this faith story?

If your congregation is well versed in all things Harry Potter, it's a great day to talk about Dumbledore. All those times when he gave Harry some small glimpse of truth—without giving away the punchline—that would sustain him for the journey ahead. In other words, Dumbledore did not get to destroy all the Horcruxes in his lifetime; but he made sure Harry had the tools, and all the pieces of the story, to accomplish the thing on his own.

Are we giving our children the right tools? And the right pieces of the story?

Communion Prayer

God, we have been to the mountaintop, and we long to stay here in your presence. But you have called us to journey on. Bless this bread, that it might sustain us for the road ahead; bless this cup, that it might be our hope in the valley; draw us close at this table, and send us out, renewed, that we might share good news with the world. Amen.

February 18, 2018–First Sunday in Lent

Passages: Genesis 9:8-17; Psalm 25:1-10; 1 Peter 3:18-22; Mark 1:9-15

Opening Prayer

God of grace and of new beginnings, drench our worship today with your Holy Spirit. Enable our every gesture of worship, imperfect though they always are, even so to redound to your glory and to make your splendor easier for all the world to see. In Christ, Amen.

Preaching Theme

The Gospel of Mark moves right along such that even just reading these verses can leave you a little breathless. The kind of narrative details someone like Luke might luxuriate in seem here to have been stripped away such that we are left with a streamlined story that wastes no time getting down to business. Jesus gets baptized and if, for a fleeting moment, we see the Spirit come down like a dove, it takes just a narrative heartbeat for that dove to transmogrify into a different kind of bird altogether. Suddenly the Spirit is more like a raptor who seizes the beloved Son of God in its talons and then fairly hurls him (the vivid verb *ekballein* in Greek) into the desert the way in old movies you see bouncers at a bar throw someone through a glass window and out onto the street. This happens—to use Mark's favorite adverb—"immediately" upon Jesus's coming out of the river of baptism.

No sooner does this happen and—despite the richness of the temptation story in Matthew and Luke—Mark tells us very simply that Jesus was in the presence of wild animals and yet angels attended him. Mark is a minimalist if ever there were one, but he knows exactly what keywords to throw in to alert biblically savvy readers as to what's happening. In scripture words seldom sound a single note on the biblical keyboard: they always form chords with other passages. Here, the chaos of the wilderness—a symbol throughout the Bible of all those forces that oppose God—is brought out with just the reference to "wild animals." The wilderness is the sign of evil, the threat to shalom, the very opposite of God's good cosmos as God created it in the beginning. But Jesus takes shalom with him wherever he goes and so transforms that wilderness into a peaceable kingdom of flourishing and life (cf. Isa 11).

Jesus was with the wild animals, but they did not harm or destroy because wherever Jesus goes, the holy mountain of God follows. So when Jesus then immediately goes into Galilee to pick up where John the Baptist left off, it is with true fervor and all the shalom-building presence of God within him that he is able to announce, "Here comes God's kingdom!"

As a passage to kick off another Lenten season, there is in Mark 1's swift strokes a profound hope. Because no sooner is Jesus confirmed in his baptism as God's beloved Son and the first order of business is to go straight at the world's most squalid places. Where else would the Messiah begin his work if not on skid row, in the hospice ward, at the cancer clinic, on the dementia unit at the nursing home? These are the places that encapsulate the chaos of sin for us. These are the wilderness places most in need of healing. Of course Jesus has to go to the chaotic wilderness first and foremost. Why else had he come?

Secondary Preaching Themes (Genesis 9)

On a pop level most people seem to think that the Genesis flood resulted from the anger and fury and wrath of God over sin. That's not what Genesis says, however. No, God was "grieved" over the state of the world he had made. He was heartsick, sad, shattered by what the people made in his own image had become. So he sends a flood but at some point realizes that this would not lead to a lasting solution. So somewhere between Genesis 6 and Genesis 9 God turns from grief to grace. Never again would he send a flood, and the rainbow would remind him and humanity of this truth.

From then on out in the Bible it's all grace all the time. The season of Lent leads us to the ultimate expression of that grace: the cross itself. God's heartbreak over sin would lead him to take all the sadness, all the tragedy of human history onto himself, and put it to death once and for all. Frankly, this was a lot harder for God to do than just letting it rain forty days and forty nights. But if the waters of that flood left too many people dead, the waters of baptism would leave untold numbers of people forever alive to God.

Benediction (from 1 Peter 3)

Now from Jesus Christ who was raised from the dead and who sits at God's right hand, and from the Father whose power raised him, and from the Holy Spirit who floods your heart with the saving waters of baptism: grace, mercy, and peace both this day and forever more. Amen.

February 25, 2018–Second Sunday in Lent

Passages: Genesis 17:1-7, 15-16; Psalm 22:23-31; Romans 4:13-25; Mark 8:31-38 (or Mark 9:2-9)

Gathering Prayer

Jesus, you save us in your resurrection, and you continue to come to us so that we might be reconciled to you. Remind us that, in our baptisms and our lives of faith, we follow your example. We embody your presence in the world, but we do not replace you. We serve you and work toward your kingdom in the world. But we still need your salvation from the beginning of our lives until their end. Remind us, so that we offer praise in our congregation because of you. Remind us, so that we act in the light of what God has done. Amen.

Preaching Theme

Even when we're close to Christ, it's easier to act like Satan. In chapter 7, Jesus basically calls a Syrophoenician mother an animal that rhymes with "witch." But in chapter 8, he insults Peter, his "rock" disciple, like no other—Get behind me, *Satan*. Why such vicious words? Scripture tells us it's because Peter thought he knew God's will better than Jesus did.

Yet who could blame Peter for revolting? Peter saw Jesus cast out demons, heal the sick, calm the sea, and raise the dead. For Peter, how could that Jesus end up executed…with resurrection promised three days later or not? Today, lesser disciples like us still find the outburst of Jesus troubling if we take it seriously.

The verses that follow make more sense—to take up our cross and follow Jesus so that we might have life. We tithe, resist materialism, champion the rights of the disenfranchised and oppressed, and befriend neighbors, strangers, and enemies with the love and mercy of God. Yet like Peter, we struggle to comprehend why we need the crucifixion and resurrection of Jesus in order to align our minds with the Christ's. The Passion sounds too far out compared to our good work on the ground. It's easier to follow what Jesus says than to place our faith in what he does.

Peter hears Jesus clearly. Yet he refuses to accept what Jesus must do for him and for all of humanity and creation. He grabs Jesus and uses him as a crutch to hold up his own self-righteousness instead of reaching for the cross to leave his theologically unimaginative ways of thinking behind and find life in the Human One. By doing so, Peter not only exchanges his life for a lie, he also becomes precisely the opposite of what he thought he was: not a disciple, but a devil in the flesh. In the second week of Lent, will we sacrifice our embarrassment about needing the crucified and resurrected Jesus? Or will we choose to work harder and harder at saving ourselves with the risk of thinking like a mere mortal or, worse, like an adversary of God?

Secondary Preaching Themes

Psalm 22:27-28

This passage states, "Every part of the earth will remember and come back to the LORD; every family among all the nations will worship you. Because the right to rule belongs to the LORD, he rules all nations." The psalmist declares that promise even though Psalm 22 begins with a cry of distress repeated by Jesus in Mark 15:34 and Matthew 27:46: "My God, my God, why have you left me?" *The psalmist understands human anguish and knows that we belong to God in the deepest realms of our despair.* Psalm 22 therefore provides an ancient root for the message interpreted above from Mark—God still saves us even when it seems as if no one cares except ourselves.

1 Peter 3:18-22

Baptism means more than a spiritual bath to cleanse the faithful of our fleshly filth. *Baptism saves us right now because, in baptism, our lives become publicly pledged to God in that sacrament.* Baptismal washing (or sprinkling), whether we can remember it or not, takes us to where Jesus is.[1] In that way, we may not be conscious of our "good conscience to God" as marked by baptism. That's okay. God does the saving that we may not clearly see or comprehend in the depths of the baptismal waters. In the season of Lent, we can ponder our forgotten and formative baptismal experiences, and bring ourselves back to a beginning shared with Christ. We can pray and return to a sacramental starting place that helps us make memories of Jesus, that we also did not witness, into our own so that we can live into the reality and future of God. Peter found God's reality unacceptable. We can wash away the potential to make the same kind of mistake by praying for the Spirit to illuminate the profundity of our baptisms.

Benediction

Go, unashamed that our faith rests upon a God become human who died and rose again. Receive the scandal of the crucifixion and the mystery of the resurrection as vanishing points to contemplate in this season of Lent. May they show how the good that we do here takes shape within the dimensions of an eternal plan. Amen.

March 4, 2018–Third Sunday in Lent

Passages: *Exodus 20:1-17; Psalm 19; 1 Corinthians 1:18-25; John 2:13-22*

Gathering Prayer

O God, when the psalmist asks, "Let the words of my mouth and the meditations of my heart be pleasing to you, LORD, my rock, and my redeemer," we might hear a trite phrase that a preacher uses before delivering a sermon. Let us hear those words again—"Let the words of my mouth and the meditations of my heart be pleasing to you, LORD, my rock, and my redeemer"—instead as a prayer of hope that we all can pray. May we find occasions to recite what the psalmist asks so that the sentences we utter and the concerns that we have are taken up into the hands of a God who gives, teaches, judges, and redeems all. Amen.

Preaching Theme

When reminiscing about the founding of his company, Alibaba, English teacher-turned-e-commerce billionaire Jack Ma essentially says again and again that the only advantage he had was being disadvantaged. As preachers of the gospel, *even when it seems as though all we have to share is our words, the infinite wisdom of God becomes known by what we say.* We may not bring justice like attorneys or activists do. We may not heal bodies like doctors or nurses; facilitate learning like educators and coaches; advance society like scientists, engineers, and professionals who work with their minds and their hands; or challenge the world like artists and performers. We may not generate wealth like Ma and entrepreneurs like him. We may not perform miracles like Jesus and the disciples, or like guardians in the home do in their everyday acts of love. Our institutions—churches, fellowships, and denominational bodies—may no longer thrive. Parishioners may find the messages that we deliver tired. Congregations may seem destined not to survive as a result of differences we cannot help reconcile.

Yet no matter how demoralizing pastoral life can be, as well as when it's great or just status quo, every sermon, including the ones that utterly fail, provides an opportunity for speaking and hearing God's eternal ken.

Divine wisdom takes shape in language, and we can grasp it. We see it in its most human form in the frustrated, counterintuitive, yet stringently practical proclamations of Jesus. "Get these things out of here! Don't make my Father's house a place of business" (John 2:16). How often have we exchanged difficult thinking about mission for preoccupation with how to accumulate and save money in congregations? Divine wisdom also makes itself known in the minutes taken by Moses after he meets with God: "You must have no other gods before me" and "Do not kill." If we have come to doubt whether the biblical witness makes sense in a greedy and violent existence like the one we must negotiate today, we can notice how scripture gives way to what the entirety of creation quietly indicates as true: "Heaven is declaring God's glory; the sky is proclaiming his handiwork. One day gushes the news to the next, and one night informs another what needs to be known" (Ps 19:1-2). What we need to know is that, even when the presence of God feels weak in our holy pages and in our preaching, the power of God's promises radiates around us.

Secondary Preaching Themes

Exodus 20:1-17

This passage presents the Ten Commandments, otherwise known as the Decalogue. The Ten Commandments articulate a "higher law." Their display and subsequent removal has roiled courtrooms like the Alabama Judicial Building, but portions of the Commandments also have gone relatively unnoticed in artworks like the south frieze of the United States Supreme Court. Incidentally, a depiction of Muhammad also appears on the north frieze with a book of Arabic script that appears to be the Quran. The Ten Commandments declared holy limits for how the Israelites should live. In his earthly ministry, Jesus came to fulfill those laws and all others in order to save the lost sheep of the house of Israel. Yet Jesus followed the Ten Commandments with ingenuity when he did not stop the disciples from eating on the Sabbath (Mark 2:23-28), and he completed his earthly mission in such a way that even a Roman centurion realized, "Truly this man was God's Son." *How will we interpret the "higher law" of God today so that we expansively share the salvation of God in places of hunger and death?*

1 Corinthians 1:18-25

Sometimes, it's all too easy to read a passage like 1 Corinthians 1:18-25, where "the foolishness of God is wiser than human wisdom," as an excuse to turn our noses up at theological education or thinking critically about what it means to be a faithful Christian. Yet Paul, the author of 1 Corinthians, a Roman citizen and Jew, fluent in Koine Greek and Hebrew, who studied "at the feet of Gamaliel" (a Pharisee "respected by all"), did not intend for his readers to think that at all (Acts 22:3; 5:34). Rather, he wanted to communicate the primacy of God's wisdom to which all of our intellectual exploration and our ignorance must answer. *Realizing how wise God is often means taking our own mental prowess to the limit.*

Benediction

May we open our minds and our mouths to the wisdom of God. Let us find strength and courage by thinking rigorously about who Jesus is for us and speaking boldly about his salvation for us now and forever. Go, with the peace of the Spirit. Amen.

Harmonizing Glory

Psalm 19

....

Jacob D. Myers

"The heavens are telling the glory of God and the firmament proclaims God's handiwork." And all God's people said, "Amen."

But ought we?

Can we truly affirm the glory of God with our frail and fallow words? Like a beautiful vista, a breathtaking sunset, human discourse fails to articulate the splendor of the Divine. Like the evanescent whispers of a dream almost remembered, the more we talk about it, the less real it becomes. In short, can the words of our mouths and the meditations of our hearts *ever* be acceptable in God's sight?

The psalmist offers us a glimpse—just a glimpse—of the impossible possibility of beholding God's glory in the physical world and in the world of Torah. Sights and sounds. Tellings and glimmers. Whispers of the luminous halo of God's glory. There! Did you see it? Did you hear it? I guess you had to be there.

Harvard theologian Mayra Rivera rightly argues that "glory is the event that lures us into the experience of wonder."[1] Thus, I think that the tellings of the heavens and the proclamations of the firmament are less like exhalations by which we receive anything from God and more like the Divine inhalation that draws us into the mystery of Godself, summoning our participation. The glory of God hollows us out. It disrupts us and destabilizes our singularity, our sovereignty, before a Lordly multiplicity.

Oh, that we would see with the psalmist's eyes and listen with his ears. The poet employs metaphor: the apprehension of identity within difference. But even as new symbols give rise to new thoughts, our words betray us, grounding us more firmly in the singular world of our experience—the tyranny of the Same. The sun, illuminating our goings and comings, is the very thing upon which we cannot directly gaze for fear of blindness. A bridegroom, the one who is already spoken for, emerges from his tent. For some this is a propitious coming, for others who have suffered domestic abuse and even marital rape, a harbinger of doom. The glory of God is like a strong man who cannot be stymied, who will not and cannot be forestalled. Fighting for us, he charges into battle. But for many who've been ravaged by war, and for those who have felt the ruthless sting of fundamentalism's scepter, the might of the strong man is the antithesis of glory Divine.

The glory of God announces itself in all its radiant mystery, in all its virile frailty. It presents itself as that which cannot be presented. It is unpresentable, and it is in its very impossibility of human articulation that it marks the limits of human possibility.

28 –

We see the psalmist's dilemma mirrored in the famous words of St. Augustine. "But when I love you, what do I love?" the African bishop asks.

> It is not physical beauty nor temporal glory nor the brightness of light dear to earthly eyes, nor the sweet melodies of all kinds of songs, nor the gentle odor of flowers and ointments and perfumes, nor manna or honey, nor limbs welcoming the embraces of the flesh; it is not these things that I love when I love my God.
>
> Yet there *is* a light I love, and a food, and a *kind* of embrace when I love my God—a light, voice, odor, food, embrace of my inner [person] where my soul is floodlit by light which space cannot contain, where there is sound that time cannot seize, where there is a perfume which no breeze disperses, where there is a taste for food no amount of eating can lessen, and where there is a bond of union that no saity can part. *That* is what I love when I love my God.[2]

We witness a similar sentiment when the psalmist declares, "There is no speech, nor are there words; their voice is not heard; **yet** their voice goes out through all the earth, and their words to the end of the world" (vv. 3–4, NRSV). Such is the glory, the blinding splendor, of God.

It is in such breathtaking simplicity that we are to reflect upon Torah, as the psalmist does in verse 7 and following. Here the psalmist says all that cannot be said by saying all he can say; indeed, it is only in transcending the limits of speech that we ever say anything about God. To hear these words in all their theological superabundance demands that we do not neglect the psalmist's earlier declarations concerning God's word revealed in its hiddenness.

> "The law of the LORD is perfect" ... *but beyond all perfection*
> "reviving the soul" *with a nourishment that empties us out.*
> "The decrees of the LORD are sure" ... *but beyond all certainty*
> "making wise the simple" *with a simplicity that transcends knowledge.*
> "The precepts of the LORD are right" ... *calling us to lives of justice beyond ethics,*
> "rejoicing the heart" *by drawing us into longing.*
> "The commandment of the LORD is clear" ... *bursting with the full spectrum*
> *of Divine possibility,*
> "enlightening the eyes" *through a luminous darkness.*
> "The fear of the LORD is pure" ... *summoning us to wonder.*
> "The ordinances of the LORD are true and righteous altogether" ... *calling each and*
> *every truth into question, along with our paltry displays of righteousness.* (NRSV)

In verse 10, the psalmist concludes his ode to Torah, declaring God's law *richer* than the purest gold and *sweeter* than the finest honey. In other words, the law of the Lord displays God's glory most fully when it leaves us feeling poor and hungry. It is then that we may follow the light of God's glory—a glory revealed in creation as well as scripture—into the world God loves. It is then that we hear the call to participate in God's justice, to embody God's righteousness.

Between the grandeur of creation and the persistence of suffering and creaturely frailty there is a hiatus, a spacing, a moment between call and response, between glory and deed. Howard Thurman describes this as a "creative isthmus of twilight joining day with night." He says, "It is the time of pause when nature changes her guard. It is the lung of time by which the rhythmic respiration of day and night are guaranteed and sustained. All living things would fade and die from too much light or too much darkness, if twilight were not."[3] With the psalmist, we must embrace the twilight, the flicker of God's radiance that is at once blinding and revealing, deafening and summoning. Only then are we able to render words into deeds, metaphors into manifestations of God's glory in and through us.

In this psalm we are called to *harmonize* with the glory of God. That's what the word *meditation* really means in verse 14. It is a musical term, whose meaning is muddled in our contemporary hearing because we are so focused on thinking and knowing.

Limited by sight. Barred from sound. Stammering and stuttering before the glory of God, the psalmist strives to bring his life into harmony with God. To consecrate the melodic union between elsewhere and everywhere demands a kind of epistemological abstinence—a "learned ignorance," Nicolas of Cusa will call it. It is a way of knowing that breaks forth into a way of being. This is what the psalmist is getting at when he prays for God to purge him of hidden faults, to guard him against his propensity to presumptuousness, to assume that the glory of God is something to be wielded. This, my friends, is the dawning of revelation, the twilight of justice.

"May the words of our mouths and the movement of our bodies harmonize with your glory, so that we may be found acceptable in your sight, O LORD, our rock and our redeemer." Amen.

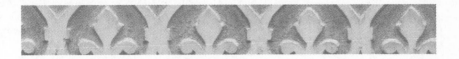

March 11, 2018—Fourth Sunday in Lent

Passages: Numbers 21:4-9; Psalm 107:1-3, 17-22; Ephesians 2:1-10; John 3:14-21

Gathering Prayer

Faithful redeemer, Psalm 107 tells us that you ordered, healed, and rescued your people "from their pit." We come to you now in the desperation of our own circumstances. In the fourth week in Lent, we sacrifice our confusion, worries, and inadequacies to you. We trust that your Spirit will renew and redeem us with unstoppable hope, no matter how much we doubt. We believe, pray, and continue in the mysterious mercy of your Son, Jesus Christ. Amen.

Preaching Theme

Ephesians tells us that you are God's accomplishment. That claim seems far from Numbers 21:4-9, where God sends poisonous snakes to punish the Israelites for their disobedience and then heals them with a bronze replica of a snake on a pole made by Moses. Yet in John 3:14-21, the serpentine episode of Numbers gets reworked to show how the relationship between God and humanity has fundamentally changed through the gift of Jesus Christ. God sends the Son not to imperil people but to save them. Jesus comes inviting us to believe and to approach the light of God by doing acts of truth. If we choose what is "evil" or what is hurtful (Greek: *ponéros*) or what is "wicked" or worthless (Greek: *phaulos*) instead (and the author of John seems to have enough confidence in the maturity of his readers that they will know for themselves what hurtful and worthless actions entail), then we choose neither the God of Numbers nor the Jesus of John but ourselves. We take what God has given us and what God desires to save—our lives—and conform it to an unremarkable path of self-destruction. A verse like Ephesians 2:3 makes the point emphatically: "All of you used to do whatever felt good and whatever you thought you wanted so that you were children headed for punishment just like everyone else." Yet God gives us the opportunity to recognize that our lives are more than what we think and what we do. We are God's "accomplishment" or God's work (Greek: *poiéma*). We have been created "to do good things" in Christ who offers ultimate and everlasting good to the world by virtue of the way he lived, died, rose, and will come again (Eph 2:10).

Secondary Preaching Themes

Ephesians 2:1-10

At the core of understanding God's mercy is the realization that salvation does not begin with us but with God. As Ephesians 2:8 underscores, the salvation Christ offers "is God's gift." Although the epistolary passage from Ephesians appears for us in the season of Lent in 2018, Wesley preached precisely the same point on June 18, 1738, at the University Church of St. Mary the Virgin in Oxford, England: "Neither is salvation of the works we do when we believe, for it is then God that worketh in us: and, therefore, that he giveth us a reward for what he himself worketh, only commendeth the riches of his mercy, but leaveth us nothing whereof to glory."[4] In other words, God's salvation does not become apparent in the good that we do, but the mercy of God given to us that then compels us to forgive and improve the world. A couple of verses earlier, verses 4-5, the point is made another way—being alive means knowing that God is rich in mercy. So, whether we find the life of faith fulfilling or feel destitute as a result of following Christ, or whether we're thin, rich, popular, and powerful, or if our health is failing, our money is tight, our relationships are broken, and our lives are strained, incoherent, and violent, God is rich in mercy. When we feel as if we're on the verge of something or the cliff of being reduced to nothing, the spirit of God offers infinite compassion to bring us to lives of goodness in Christ that happen now and last forever.

Numbers 21:4-9

God ultimately desires to heal the people of God. It's hard to make sense of God sending biting snakes to punish the Israelites in Numbers 21:4-9. The passage states why: the Israelites spoke against *God* and Moses. Yet the divine reaction seems extreme. Perhaps a larger takeaway is how the author of Numbers draws from ancient Near Eastern appreciation of the serpent as both venomous and virile to illuminate the ultimate desire of God to heal.[5] The people speak against God. Yet when God finally responds in words following the repentance of the Israelites and the intercession of Moses, he instructs Moses to counter the poison of the biting snakes with a new creation—a bronze snake on a wand that restores life upon the wounded who look to it. In Christianity, the action of Moses indicates the crucifixion of Jesus, except that in Christ there is no separation between "good" and "bad"; in his death and resurrection, he welcomes all that humans are. If we look to Jesus, whether we are wounded by ourselves, one another, "by God," or seemingly not at all, we also can live into the eternal healing of Jesus.

Benediction

You are God's accomplishment. God has made you and saved you to do good things. Yet no matter what we do—the good, the bad, the ugly, the beautiful, or something in between— life begins with the wealth of God's mercy, and we can always and in any circumstance forgive as extravagantly as God does. Amen.

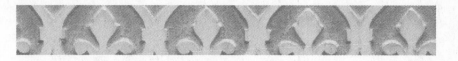

March 18, 2018–Fifth Sunday in Lent

Passages: Jeremiah 31:31-34; Psalm 51:1-12 (or Psalm 119:9-16); Hebrews 5:5-10; John 12:20-33

Gathering Prayer

Loving God, empower us to think about your precepts and examine all your paths, so that we might, like the psalmist in 119, delight in your statutes and not forget what you have said. As we contemplate and remember you, may your Spirit consider and remember us. May it enliven our worship with joy, thanksgiving, and fortitude in the gospel promise that everyone will be drawn to you. All these things we pray in Christ's name. Amen.

Preaching Theme

Even Jesus didn't want to die. In the Gospel of John, Jesus speaks with resolve about his impending death. On the one hand, he is "deeply troubled." On the other hand, he understands that "for this is the reason I have come to this time." In other words, it's as if he's thinking, "Let's do this!" Yet the author of Hebrews seems a little more real. He makes the point that Jesus appeals to God with loud cries and tears. Only through God's faithfulness to him and his devotion to God was Jesus able to sacrifice his anxiety and himself in order to "become the source of eternal salvation to everyone who obeys him." In the extraordinary gift of his life that results in his resurrection and eternal life for all who believe in him, Christ not only knits human finitude to the infinite grace of God, but he also becomes a priest of an eternal order.

Secondary Preaching Themes

Hebrews 5:5-10

The author of Hebrews draws upon the legend of Melchizedek to elucidate how *Jesus is a priest with pastoral power that lasts forever, even though Jesus fears his crucifixion.* Genesis 14:17-20 introduces Melchizedek as a king and a priest of "El Elyon"—the

Supreme God who blesses Abram and to whom Abram pays one-tenth of all he has just before God tells Abram he will have as many children as the stars (Gen 15:5). Because Abraham gave an offering to Melchizedek, and Melchizedek is a priest of "El Elyon" and a "priest forever" (Ps 110:4), Melchizedek is elevated as greater than Abraham in the eyes of the author of Hebrews. Moreover, for the author of Hebrews, Melchizedek represents a priestly line that leads to Jesus. Just as Melchizedek's priesthood stands in every era within the Bible, so, too, does Christ's. Yet the priesthood of Jesus supersedes the priest of "El Elyon" because Jesus deserves absolute worship, and not just a tithe, as he embodies eternal salvation from God for all of humankind.[6]

Jeremiah 31:31-34

God's new covenant speaks to all. In Jeremiah 31:31-34, God promises the people of Israel and Judah that God will make an entirely new covenant with them and put it within them and engrave it upon their hearts. The covenant of Sinai that was broken (Ex 19–Num 11) will be restored by God, and God will make the new covenant equally available to all of God's chosen people.[7] The passage is the only instance in the Old Testament or Hebrew Bible where "new covenant" [ברית חדשה] appears.[8] Therefore it marks a significant shift in the relationship between God and the families of Israel. Many interpret Jeremiah to mean that the new covenant of God becomes internalized as opposed to externally declared in law that the families of Israel continuously failed to follow. For a commentator like William L. Holladay, however, the "within" refers to a city of God and the "heart" is the temple within that city.[9] Jeremiah's portrait of God's promise then concerns not only the people of God but also the places where they lived and the houses in which they worshipped. For Christian preachers today who connect the relationship between Christ and humanity to the intimacy promised by God to the exilic families of Israel, Jeremiah 31:31-34 becomes unusually versatile as a portrait of divine faithfulness. If Christian preachers take care not to confuse the passage as Christian, Jeremiah's pivotal portrait of divine promise for the families of Israel provides a way of imagining how Christ comprehensively restores the brokenness of our lives in all of their individual, collective, societal, and congregational complexity.

Benediction

Let us embrace the Christ who suffered and died as more than an invincible memory that distracts us from the pain of the world. Let us receive the Christ who suffered and died as more than an allegorical figure who gives reason for our sacrificial service to others. Let us receive the Christ as a lucid reality whose Spirit shines through our acts of courageous generosity, undeserved love, and unverifiable faith to bring light to the world and glory to God. Amen.

March 25, 2018–Palm and Passion Sunday

Passages: Liturgy of the Palms: Psalm 118:1-2, 19-29; Mark 11:1-11; Passion Sunday: Isaiah 50:4-9a; Psalm 31:9-16; Philippians 2:5-11; Mark 14:1–15:47

Liturgy for the Procession of the Palms

One: Hosanna! Blessed is the one who comes in the name of the Lord.

All: Hosanna! Blessed are those who come with praise.

One: Blessed are those who come in numbers

All: Blessed are they who enter alone.

One: Blessed are those who will lay down their cloaks,

All: Blessed are those who will lay down their arms.

One: Blessed are those who know, who believe,

All: Blessed are they who doubt, who wonder.

One: We come with the hopes and the fears of the world.

All: We come with our own longing, our own things to lay down.

One: Shout Hosanna, and come as one.

All: Sing Hosanna, and come in praise.

Preaching Theme

There's Mark's favorite word again: "immediately."

This Gospel of so few words uses "immediately" more than forty times. Like the rhythm of the story itself, this use of language contributes to the overall urgency of the movement. As the narrative moves closer to the events of Holy Week, that sense of immediacy seems all the more amplified.

Time is short. What are we going to do with it?

There's a certain tension around the events of Palm Sunday that is unmatched by any other day on the liturgical calendar. A day that starts with festivity and celebration and a parade of children ends with a question mark hanging over the gathered crowd. We know what's coming next. We know what the coming days might bring.

This version of the entry story plays to that tension, its resolution open-ended as Jesus exits stage right with the disciples. They are bound for Bethany—and we know what comes next. I've made it a habit to incorporate that tension into the sermon, and into the liturgy itself, on Palm Sunday. It's a day for holding the tension between that which is inevitable, and that which might still be changed, if we hurry; a day to hold the ecstatic crowd alongside the gathering darkness; a day to end with a question, maybe even an uncomfortable silence, instead of a benediction and assurance of peace.

If we can effectively draw that tension into the service, then the sermon need not be long or complex. And there will always be a story in the newsfeed—perhaps more recent, more uncomfortably close to home than we'd like—to illustrate the power of mob mentality; and how quickly that gathered crowd can turn from ecstatic to murderous, like a quick change in the weather. Where will we be the next time that wind blows?

Secondary Preaching Themes (Mark 14:1-15:47)

Instead of the Liturgy of the Palms, some churches choose this day to explore the Passion narrative. Rather than the open-ended mystery of the previous episode, this passage follows—in long and painful detail—the journey from triumphal entry to betrayal, suffering, and death.

It is a long passage, when taken all at once, and would be a difficult one to preach with integrity. The key is to choose one element of this story and explore it in a way that illuminates the whole. If your church gathers for Maundy Thursday, you'll want to save the Last Supper for that service. If your people gather to observe Good Friday, then you want to save the darkness of the cross for that day.

Perhaps Passion Sunday, then, is a day to explore deeply the pain of betrayal; the sin of placing our faith in human institutions and expressions of power, rather than in the God who has earned our trust; and the baser impulses that, time and again, lead even well-meaning people to turn from what is right and good, and cling to that which is easy or profitable.

Benediction

We do not leave in peace today. Our spirits are unsettled.

There is no closing circle, no comforting word. Our hearts are restless.

We carry no lamp as we bear witness to the gathering darkness.

We draw close. We watch. And we wait.

March 29, 2018–Maundy Thursday

*Passages: Exodus 12:1-4 (5-10), 11-14; Psalm 116:1-2, 12-19;
1 Corinthians 11:23-26; John 13:1-17, 31b-35*

Gathering Prayer

God, who calls us to remember by giving signs, symbols, movements, and stories. We your people long to live into our promised future, our call to be agents of your love, our call to give of ourselves like you have done again and again. Help us lean into memory as we gather on this holy day. May the water, the bread, the wine, the towel, and the oil make present for us your love, your call, and our hope. All of this we ask in the name of our remembered, Jesus Christ our Lord. Amen.

Preaching Theme

The Exodus reading is the perfect beginning of the dramatic story that will unfold in the next three days. It is filled with such beautiful images: food, people gathering, blood, fear, and redemption. This is the stuff that great stories are made of, this is the stuff of life!

At the center of it all, of all the imagery, instruction, and speed, is a call to remember. We are to proclaim, to pay attention, to tell the story again and again. To teach this story to our children, and our children's children; to make sure that each generation knows that this is their story. They too finding new life, they too being freed from slavery, they too being heard by God, they too being handed down a word from the Lord, they too having their feet washed and called to serve.

The narratives today are extremely vivid so that we do not forget. A community being freed after generations in slavery, a God who hears the cry of those who needed most, a set of words that have been "received," and a master and Savior who kneels down and reminds the followers to do likewise. Remember, remember, remember…

It is easy on Holy/Maundy Thursdays to go through the motions. We have been here before, the story is the same, often the congregants are too. Yet we must find a way on this day to capture the drama, power, and hope of remembering.

Today, let's dig deep and find ways for the stories we share today to become our stories. How can we experience freedom today? How can we experience a God who hears us when we cry? How can we experience the passing on of this tradition? How can we get our feet washed, our whole bodies, in preparation to become love givers in the world?

As we gather at the beginning of a series of commemorations, how can we as God's people remember, bring back into being, make this amazing story our story? Remember, remember, remember!

Secondary Preaching Themes

The Gospel today is deeply rooted in incarnate practice! I can feel the water on my toes, I can feel hands soaping them up, rinsing them, and drying them with a warm towel. I can feel my clean feet ready for a clean and dry pair of socks. I can hear Jesus telling me to do likewise.

Again and again we are told to practice what we have been told. Not just to be observers, voyeuristically looking in without a willingness to get in the middle of it. But participants who "lift up the cup," keep promises made, prepare meals, and are ready to go where sent.

I wonder if it might be a perfect time to speak to the congregation about the connection between remembrance and practice? How can we help our people recognize the importance of repetition, posture, and witness in our formation as disciples and in the ways that we help a new generation of God's people to be shaped and formed in the stories that shape our identity?

Another related theme is tradition and its role in our daily life and in our faith. If a culture seems to be averse to tradition or traditional things, it might be helpful on this day as we begin the great drama of our salvation to speak about the power and importance of tradition as remembering practice.

Responsive Reading (based on Psalm 116)

I love the Lord because he hears my request for mercy.

I'll call out to him as long as I live, because he listens closely to me.

When death comes and distress comes near.

I'll call out to him, because he listens closely to me.

When I need protection because I've been brought down.

I'll call out to him, because he listens closely to me.

When my eyes are teary, my feet stumbling, and death near.
I'll call out to him, because he listens closely to me.

Now I keep my promise, give back, and remain God's servant.
I'll call out to him, because he listens closely to me.

Benediction

People of God, remember:

Love each other,

As Jesus loved you,

That is the way that all people will know

The good news of God's kingdom.

Now go with the blessing of God,

Who is Father, Son, and Holy Spirit.

March 30, 2018–Good Friday

Passages: Isaiah 52:13–53:12; Psalm 22; Hebrews 10:16-25 or Hebrews 4:14-16; 5:7-9; John 18:1–19:42

Gathering Prayer

Suffering God, you became one of us, taking our shame, guilt, and sin. As we walk in these days, make us deeply aware of the suffering around us, in our homes, our neighborhoods, our cities and towns. By the power of your Holy Spirit, make us deeply attentive to the forgotten, the lost, lonely, oppressed, denied, mocked, and afflicted. May the sacrifice of your Son save us as others see salvation through us; through Christ our Lord, Amen.

Preaching Theme

In the church we often struggle to talk about that which is ugly, undesirable, to be avoided, that which our human nature is trained to ignore. How often do we look away at the difficult: someone with a physical impairment that makes them unsightly, a rundown neighborhood, a pile of garbage, a dead body, a homeless person.

We are wired to look away, to ignore, to move on, and to drive off in a hurry. We are wired to not be uncomfortable.

Today's readings from Isaiah to the Gospel force us to face the reality of suffering. We have a suffering servant who is disfigured, inhuman, crushed, tormented, afflicted, sick, and despised. A Savior, who is struck, denied, stripped, whipped, mocked, and bleeding. A psalmist, who feels abandoned, betrayed, rejected, and despised, by others and by God.

On Good Friday we have an opportunity to ponder the unsightliness of salvation. We must help our congregations get comfortable with uncomfortableness, become at ease with uneasiness, and be willing to look at unsightliness.

The sacrifice of Jesus on the cross and the sacrifice asked of us as disciples is difficult, uncomfortable, and unavoidable. The good news is that as the prophet reminds us "by his wounds we are healed." That by the recognition of our own pain, brokenness, and suffering and by our becoming allies with all who are despised, oppressed, and tormented we too are healed again and again.

Even more, by our participation and our paying attention even when difficult, we can begin to be agents of healing, reconciliation, and restoration of all of creation.

So preacher, lean on the disfigured, avoided, and crushed. On this day may the woundedness become a source of new life for all who gather.

Secondary Preaching Themes

Hebrews gives us some interesting fodder on Good Friday when it reminds us that God will not remember our sin. ·

Remembering is easy these days! We, young and old alike, constantly track our every move. We take pictures, check in, post status updates, and share our locations. Our every move seems to be easily tracked and easily remembered. Employers look over our Facebook feeds as part of the hiring processes, our youthful indiscretions easily marking us for life. Why does God choose to forget when the rest of the world desperately seeks to remember?

The ugly, disfigured, undesirable is easy to remember. Many of the viral videos are the most heinous. You have heard the expression "It's like watching a train wreck." Who is this God that easily forgets our "train wreck" moments? The moments in our life and in the life of our communities that no one is proud of but everyone obsesses over. Hebrews reminds us that if we are in Christ we then are agents of that new beginning so that we too do not remember and instead we "without wavering… encourage each other."

How is the cross and the death of Jesus a pathway to a new start? To a place where our past does not haunt our future? What are some of the key characteristics of God that allow God to "not remember"?

Congregational Prayer (based on Psalm 22)

Gracious God, we cry out on this day,

we are ready for night to stop,

and for a new day to dawn.

Our God, our God, why have you forsaken us?

Our ancestors trusted you,

cried out to you,

and they were not ashamed.

Our God, our God, why have you forsaken us?

On this day we come alongside the forgotten,

the despised, the mocked, the insulted,

we align ourselves with the undesirables of our world.

Our God, our God, why have you forsaken us?

God, hear us!

Our sin, shame, and guilt surround us,

like lions they threaten to consume us!

Our God, our God, why have you forsaken us?

Save us, O God!

we trust that by your wounds we are healed,

that you listen when we cry for help!

Our God, our God, you have not forsaken us.

Benediction

Go now, the night has come,

Go now, the day has ended,

Go now, the lots have been cast,

Go now, the veil has been torn,

Go now, it is completed!

April 1, 2018–Easter Sunday

Passages: Acts 10:34-43 (or Isaiah 25:6-9); Psalm 118:1-2, 14-24;
1 Corinthians 15:1-11 (or Acts 10:34-43); John 20:1-18 (or Mark 16:1-8)

Gathering Prayer

God of resurrection, new life, and victory over death. We your people praise you for the life-giving work that you have done through your Son, Jesus Christ. By the power of the Holy Spirit, empower us to be agents of new life, help us point all people toward the risen Lord, and may we become preparers of bounty feasts in our communities. Through Christ our Lord, Amen.

Preaching Theme

He told us he would rise again. Jesus said it, talked about it, and used parables and metaphor to remind us. Yet as the Gospel of Mark reminds us, the women were startled when they encountered the tomb. In fact even after the young man reminded them, we are told that they were "overcome with terror and dread."

Easter Sunday gathers the community like no other Lord's Day in the year. Families gather, matriarchs arrive early to reserve pews, the choir loft is full, and new clothes are worn. It is a special and exciting day! Terror and dread are not even close to the words we think about for this day.

I wonder if we have lost something along the way. Have we heard the story so much that we are no longer awed by it, curious about it, or maybe even a bit terrified of it?

Easter gives us an opportunity to engage people in the power and awe that resurrection communicates. The creator of the universe choosing to become one of us then dying and rising so that death is finally defeated! So that we, and all of creation, can be restored, redeemed, and renewed. Just the thought of it brings me to silence!

This Easter I wonder what it would be like to commit to having a conversation with the congregation about the ways that our encounters with the holy, with the power of the resurrection, might scare us into silence.

Maybe it's a witness of joy in the midst of unspeakable grief, the courage of an outcast showing up on an Easter Sunday, or the perseverance of one who's been rejected over and over again. There it is, resurrection before us, do we miss it because it is not lilies, new clothes, and family?

Let us look, let us pay attention; the resurrected Lord is often not where we expect. That reality drives us to silence, because it makes us afraid.

Secondary Preaching Themes

The book of Acts reminds us that we are witnesses to the resurrection. We are the ones given the task of telling others about the story of our salvation. We are taking the opportunity to tell others of our own encounter and experience with the risen Lord. Easter gives us the opportunity to share the many ways we can be witnesses to the risen Lord today.

Being a witness requires us learning the story, as the book of Acts reminds us "the prophets testify about him" (v. 43). This should not surprise us, for from the very beginning God has been laying out a pathway for our redemption.

Witnessing requires our courage. It is hard to tell others about our experiences with God. We get shy, don't know what to say, and might even become fearful of what others might say—could this be why the women were stunned to silence?

No matter what, we as preachers have an opportunity here to share with all who gather on this day some examples of where we have seen the resurrected Jesus at work, including how we have encountered him in our own lives. In other words, the preacher models being a witness; we like Peter, sharing what we really are learning.

Responsive Reading (based on Isaiah 25)

The Lord has prepared a feast for all people,

a rich feast, with the best food and drink.

This is the Lord, for whom we have waited;

let's be glad and rejoice in his salvation!

The Lord has removed the veil from all people,

the shroud that has kept the nations from seeing.

This is the Lord, for whom we have waited;

let's be glad and rejoice in his salvation!

The Lord has swallowed up death from all people,

the penalty for our sin has been swallowed up forever.

This is the Lord, for whom we have waited;

let's be glad and rejoice in his salvation!

The Lord has wiped off the tears from all people,

the people's disgrace from the whole earth.

This is the Lord, for whom we have waited;

let's be glad and rejoice in his salvation!

Benediction (based on 1 Corinthians 15)

I pass on to you as most important

what I also received:

Christ died for our sins

he was buried,

and he rose on the third day.

This is what we preach,

this is what you have believed,

and of this we are witnesses!

Why Are You Weeping?

John 20:1-18

Luke A. Powery

Mary Magdalene has forgotten that it is Easter. According to one writer, there are three essential prayers—help, thanks, and wow (Anne Lamott).[1] Easter is supposed to be a wow Sunday. Right? Can I have a few witnesses to say "wow"? But, Mary makes it a woe-is-me Sunday, not a wow Sunday. Come on, Mary, don't rain on our Easter parade today or dampen the mood of our party. Don't wrinkle our frilly dresses or mess up our new fancy hairdos or crush our favorite white Easter lilies. O, Mary, don't you weep. But that's exactly what she does "early on the first day of the week, while it was still dark." Mary "stood weeping outside the tomb" in a pool of tears that drench this story. One commentator says that this biblical text is "awash in tears" (Allen Callahan). The pages of the pericope are still seemingly moist with Good Friday sorrow. But it is trumpet-tongued, brass-blasting Easter at Duke Chapel! Yet Mary reveals that we are an Easter people living in a Good Friday world. Mary "stood weeping outside the tomb." Weeping is more than tears; it includes wailing and lamentation for the dead. It's an ancient Jewish expression of mourning and grief.

Why does Mary weep? She says, "They have taken away my Lord, and I don't know where they've put him." Mary does not weep as a sign of the penitence of the gift of tears, nor does she weep over the bitter division in this country over human equality. Mary weeps because she mourns the loss of Jesus. The God she knew is gone. I did not say she mourned the death of Jesus in this case, because Jesus was already dead. She weeps because Jesus is lost. The One, who declared his university major to be finding the lost, was lost himself, and she couldn't find him. Her weeping, or what John Donne calls "fruits of much grief,"[2] flow because of the presence of the absence of Jesus. Jesus is MIA, missing in action. Mary had gone to the tomb because that was where she was used to finding Jesus, the dead Jesus, the impotent Jesus, the Jesus-who-does-not-meddle-in-my-life-Jesus, comfortable and cozy Jesus. Mary had become used to the place of death, so she weeps because what she had come to expect had shifted all of the sudden and everything she knew, Jesus, was gone. She weeps due to a nostalgic disorientation.

"They have taken away my Lord, and I don't know where they've put him." Mary still expects to find a dead Jesus in a dark tomb, located in the same old place and acting in the same old way. Controlled, cold, numb, and locked in a grave cave. Mary has forgotten that it is Easter. She weeps because she has lost what she has known to be reality, the usual place where she thought she could find Jesus forever—in a mausoleum manger. "They have taken away *my* Lord," my personal Jesus, my concept of who Jesus is. I wish I could return to the days when it was as simple as "Jesus is the answer," a simpler way, no complexity to theology, no unanswered questions because the "Bible tells me so," the good ole days when I ruled God from the throne of my own anxiety, and wrapped an entombed Jesus, not in swaddling clothes, but in a psychological safety blanket. That dead Jesus was gone for Mary. Where she left him, he could no longer be found. The Jesus she knew and believed in was lost, the tame Jesus of her childhood, the one with blond hair, blue eyes, and a pointy nose on the fans used in the country church. Her Jesus, her Lord, was lost. The one she understood. The dead Jesus lying in a dead place. A Good Friday world for an Easter people.

This is in stark contrast to what Anne Lamott dreams about in her book *Plan B: Further Thoughts on Faith*.[3] She dreams of an Easter like the resurrection vision of a child in Sunday school who drew an Easter Bunny, not Mary, outside of the empty tomb, joining eternal life with a basket full of chocolate eggs. With that vision, the tomb would be tasty. Yummy yummy to my tummy. What an Easter it would be—chocolate, white chocolate with macadamia nuts, dark chocolate melted over strawberries, Hershey's chocolate ice cream cake, chocolate-covered grits with scrambled eggs. Maybe or maybe not. Either way, scientists have argued for years how eating sweet chocolate makes us feel good and is more pleasurable than listening to your favorite music or winning the lottery or even falling in love (don't let your significant other know that secret!). Chocolate can lift you to heights you've never seen before, they say. And a 2012 article in the *New England Journal of Medicine* argues that chocolate consumption contributes to one becoming a Nobel Prize winner; with this theory, we probably have a house full of Nobel Laureates![4]

Anne Lamott dreams of a chocolaty Easter—innocent, childlike, and care-free full of chocolate fountains flowing deep and wide outside of the tomb with the Easter bunny as the doorman. This is a dream. Not the reality she knows. On the contrary, she's not surprised by Mary's weeping in a Good Friday world.

Mary, not the Easter bunny, stood outside the tomb, without a basket full of chocolate eggs, but carrying despair and hope in the chest of her heart. Mary weeps because she finds herself in a Good Friday predicament on Easter morning. What else can she do in this situation? She could post a jazzy and flashy neon-colored flyer with Jesus's picture on it and put "Missing" at the top and hang it outside of the Bryan Center; but how could she do that when it seems as if Mary doesn't even know what Jesus looks like anymore? She had lost Jesus or at least her conception of him. She had gotten so used to a dead Jesus that a living Jesus was a stranger to her.

And how strange this is when Mary learns how to weep from Jesus who wept at the tomb of Lazarus. She picks up where he left off—weeping. Mary loves Jesus, and her tears are signs of that grieving love. But maybe the flood of tears blinds her eyes so she doesn't recognize Jesus when Jesus asks her face to face, "Woman, why are you crying? Who are you looking for?" She "saw Jesus standing there, but she didn't know it was Jesus." She sees him but doesn't see him with the eyes of faith. You can love someone, but once that person changes you may not recognize him or her anymore. They may be so different because death and life are different. A dead Jesus is distinct from a living Jesus. UNC's men's basketball is different from Duke's men's basketball, and we know who's dead and who's still alive in the tournament! Jesus had changed clothes because he was alive and shook off the sting of death's designer attire. Death's clothing won't fit on a living God. Jesus left his tomb linen suit in the deathbed of the grave and was now wearing living clothes of light.

The question "Who are you looking for?" suggests that the real issue was that Mary was looking for the wrong Jesus, a powerless dead Jesus in a cold tomb, just lying there. Not a living risen Jesus and Lord. She doesn't recognize him because she wasn't used to a living risen Jesus. She looked for him in the wrong places and had gotten used to a God who lies dead, inactive. A small, lifeless Jesus she could control and even carry around as she offers to take him away, if she can find out where he lays. But the living Jesus looks right at her.

Then Comedy Central arrives in the midst of a tragic time. After Jesus asks her why she's weeping and who she's looking for, Mary speaks to him "thinking he was the gardener." She's talking to the incarnate God but thinks he's a gardener. That's like walking around in a department store shopping and someone asks you if you know what row the Clorox bleach is on; and you weren't even wearing an employee name tag. What made Mary think that Jesus was a gardener? Was it his tattered clothes or his accent or his humble demeanor or his skin color or his body odor? Was it that he resembled God in the garden of Eden? Was it the sweat on his brow or the scars on his hands? A gardener? That's like someone saying to me, "You look like a preacher." What's that supposed to mean!? You can't always judge a book by its cover. The writer of Hebrews teaches us not to neglect showing hospitality to strangers because by doing so some have entertained angels without knowing it. Mary was entertaining the resurrected God but she didn't know it. She saw a gardener.

According to various accounts, Sir Winston Churchill did not have the greatest relationship with his parents. As a young boy, he was berated by his father and told that he would grow up to be a failure. They perceived him to be less than what he was. What they saw, he was not. On top of that, he had a speech impediment and was discouraged by some of his teachers; sadly, most of us have probably had a teacher or a school counselor like that, who only knew how to be a midwife for stillborn hope. Yet, Churchill became one of the major twentieth-century leaders in the world. You can't judge a book by its cover. Too small. Too big. Too tall. Too short. Too thick. Too thin. Too loud. Too soft. Too uneducated. Too unsophisticated. Too human to be divine.

Jesus can be right in front of us but we don't recognize him because we think he's just a yard maintenance man. Our lack of recognition keeps us weeping in the dark of dawn. Even when resurrection comes, we may not recognize it because we've become so used to, so familiar with crucifixions, dying, and death. And as the psychologists have taught, familiarity breeds liking. Liking death can become the norm when we hold membership at the Jerusalem temple of the tomb. Those who attend services there are dead too among the saintly zombies or at least counting down to the date of their death on the website, deathclock.com. No wonder weeping occurs. That is, weeping over our own death. Perhaps Mary weeps because a part of her dies when Jesus died. I don't know but I do know that she weeps because of disorientation due to losing her Jesus, the dead Jesus. But she's the one who's really lost because she doesn't know resurrection when it's even staring her in the face.

Good Friday weeping on Easter intrigues me, but I guess it makes sense since my former students at Princeton Seminary used to call me the "doctor of death." Mary's weeping is fascinating and I wonder something else about her weeping. Unwittingly perhaps, Mary weeps even as a deep yearning for the return of Christ. In fact, she weeps for resurrection and as a summons, an invocation for the presence of the risen Lord. She doesn't know this but her tears are prayers. Sometimes we cry and we don't even know why. We're weeping for resurrection. And just as "at the tomb of Lazarus, [Jesus's] tears inaugurated the triumph of life over death. So too, tears inaugurate the triumph of life over death here" (Callahan). In this context, we are reminded of the words of Jesus, "I am the resurrection and the life" (John 11:25).

Jesus, the one who rises and calls us by name ("Mary!") even if we don't recognize him, even if we think he's still dead. He's calling you. The risen, living Jesus refuses to be imprisoned in death's solitary confinement. This living Jesus cannot be controlled by our theological paradigms or ecclesial traditions embalmed in a tomb. We won't find the living Lord of light there, dressed in death's dingy clothes. Jesus is alive and on the move in the world, which is why he tells Mary, "Do not hold on to me." You can't control me. You can't hold me down or hold me back or keep me dead and useless. There's too much work to do in the world. Too much interceding and healing and comforting and reconciling. Bringing peace in the midst of conflict. Love where there is hatred. Justice where there is oppression. "Do not hold on to me" with your sanctified straightjacket. Release me for the work of redemption. To ascend to the Father in order to lift you higher. Don't look for me at the tomb. You'll look for me and I'll be gone. I'm not there. I won't bring you back to the way it was because I'm no longer dead. "The way out of the darkness is only by moving ahead" (Craig Barnes) into my resurrection light.[5] Don't dwell on the memories of the past, but remember the future I have for you.

Why are you weeping? Mary weeps not because she fears death but because she fears life, the new adventurous, unpredictable, resurrected life and future in Christ. The old, lost, dead, predictable, comfortable ways—dead Jesus— had passed away. Behold, the living Jesus was making all things new. Weeping for all things new. A new start, a new beginning, a new day, when there would be no more tragedy and agony. All things new. What we see in the flesh of the risen Lord is God's embodied promise that a new day has begun in Christ and that resurrections still happen. All things new. A new start with your family that had fallen apart. A new job when you've just lost a job. A new dream for your life when you thought all you were capable of were nightmares. A new medical invention that may actually help cure cancer. All things new.

Because Jesus got up, we can get up, as he lifts us up as he ascends to the Father. Mary was down but when Jesus calls her name he lifts her spirit up, he wakes her up, he resurrects her, which is why she had been weeping for resurrection all along. Mary hoped for all things new. Mary's weeping ceases in the presence of the resurrected Christ who resurrects her when he calls her name. She was dead but in that moment he made her alive. She no longer needed a dead Jesus because the living one was right in front of her. Mary had "seen the Lord" and her life was never the same again. She became an apostle to the apostles. After all she had been through in the past, this was an unexpected future.

We can't control the future but Christ leads us into the future and holds the future. We can't hold on to him because he's actually holding us. Why are you weeping? O Mary, don't you weep, mothers don't you weep, fathers don't you weep, sons don't you weep, daughters don't you weep, students don't you weep, faculty don't you weep, facility workers don't you weep, coaches don't you weep, university administrators and staff don't you weep. Because in the life of the risen Christ we pass from death to life, from death's tomb to God's triumph, from an old age to the inauguration of a new one. An age when "[God] will wipe every tear from [our] eyes." An age when "death will be no more; mourning and crying and pain will be no more." An age when we just might have chocolate for breakfast, lunch, and dinner.

Mary had forgotten Easter in her Good Friday world. But she no longer weeps, and we no longer have to sing, "O Mary, don't you weep." For weeping may endure for the night, but Easter joy comes in the morning. This morning. Jesus is not dead. He is alive. I told you it was a wow Sunday. Christ is risen. He is risen indeed. Not even Easter bunny chocolate can beat that. Alleluia!

April 8, 2018

Passages: Acts 4:32-35; Psalm 133; 1 John 1:1–2:2; John 20:19-31

Gathering Prayer

God of surprise, you who appear to us when least expected and call us to a life unforeseen, help us pay attention to the continual presence of the resurrected Lord in our homes, in our communities, and in our hearts. Help us become willing to risk life together, the sharing of our resources, and the asking of difficult questions. By the power of your Holy Spirit continue to shape us in the promised hope of resurrection, through Christ our Lord, Amen.

Preaching Theme

Life together, life in common, life in community is difficult, messy, and transformative. It sounds beautiful when we read about it in scripture or when we see naïve depictions of it in television and movies. Just the portrayals of it and our reading about it warm our hearts; we nod, cheer, and hope.

Then we show up to church for a meeting, for learning, or for worship and we are quickly disappointed. We could keep the fantasy if we did not really get involved. It is easier if all we do is attend worship and quickly make our way to our cars for lunch. But the moment that we start to meddle, that we begin to care more deeply, and that we lean toward the invitation of incarnation, well, it's complicated!

Eastertide gives us an opportunity to challenge our faith communities to be community; to become inspired at the prospects of sharing life with others, not just other believers but with neighbors, friends, and family. What does it mean to be witnesses to the resurrection? A loving life together!

Yes, it's messy, difficult, and at times it might even seem impossible. There are going to be those who are more apt to share of what they have and others who rather just observe. There are going to be those who just believe and those who will need assurances and proof. There are going to be those who sin more boldly and those who seem to get the hang of the sanctified life more easily.

Living an eastered life is living toward flourishing together. We trying again and again to love, care, connect, share, and become more human. We trying and failing to share God's love in obvious and incarnate ways. We as eastered people shining a light on the ways that the resurrected Jesus is still at work in the world. Not just in our feeble attempts at community but also in our robust exercise of our shared life.

We living resurrection together, eastering encounters along the way!

Secondary Preaching Themes

Although difficult to speak about in churches and a hot-button issue in our society, I think on this Sunday we have an opportunity to speak about what it means for a community to hold "everything in common."

So often in our culture today our possessions own us. We hoard resources and demonize those that do not have much. We rent spaces to store our extra, buy larger homes, and are always looking for the next upgrade. In church we tend to do the same, wanting more buildings, wanting our comfort, and leaning on personal preference over common good.

How can we regain the language of shared life? How can we on this Sunday speak about living toward the common good in our homes, churches, and communities? How does our encounter with the risen Lord affect our civil life?

Part of eastering the world is living in sharing communities.

Another eastering opportunity is in confession. As 1 John reminds us, we must be willing to acknowledge the ways that we are not living into our encounter with the risen Lord. Only then can we become open to the forgiving grace of God. This second Sunday of Easter we could engage our congregations in a rhythm of confession and pardon around the ways that we do not live as Easter people and the ways that we fail to witness the eastering of the world.

Prayer of Confession (based on 1 John)

God of light, you are the one who we have seen, touched, and heard. In Jesus you have shown us yourself and you have called us to fellowship to one another.

Yet we have not lived into your call. Again and again we have turned toward darkness instead of the light. We have lied to ourselves, to you, and to others. We have broken fellowship and have denied our need to be restored. We have ignored the needs of those around us, hoarded our possessions, ignored the needy in our communities, and have not been willing to live into the common good.

Forgive us, we pray. Lead us into the light. Restore our fellowship with one another and with you. Help us let go of our possessions, be willing to share them with one another, and work together so that all people can see the light of your Son, our Savior, and the resurrected Lord. It is in his name we pray, Amen.

April 15, 2018

Passages: Acts 3:12-19; Psalm 4; 1 John 3:1-7; Luke 24:36b-48

Call to Worship

Come, worship the author of life.

Come, worship the righteous God.

Come as God's children, for that is what we are.

Know this: the Lord takes personal care of the faithful.

The Lord will hear us when we cry out to him.

Come, worship the Lord.

Preaching Theme

In Acts 3:12-19, Peter addresses the people with a message that is unapologetically strong. He rightly accuses them of rejecting God and killing Jesus, the very author of life. His words are confrontational and could be interpreted as judgmental and condemning, if we fail to see that his end goal is for the people to have their sins wiped away and to enjoy a restored relationship with God (cf. verse 19). Is this not God's desire as well?

Many times we believe that loving ourselves and others means that we must not acknowledge sin. But sin in our lives should not be ignored. In order for us to respond rightly to our sin, we must first recognize it. The psalmist prays for God to search his heart to see if there is any wicked way in him. We need God's help and perspective as we search our own hearts—to think hard and even weep over our sin as Psalm 4:4 suggests. Sin is not pleasant to encounter in our lives, but we must face it head on for sin is rebellion against God, as 1 John 3:4 states clearly.

After we recognize our own sin, we must not make excuses. In Acts 3:17 Peter acknowledges that the people acted in ignorance. There is grace and understanding in this statement. But in Acts 3 ignorance does not excuse sin nor does it release people from the consequences or a need to respond. Notice that it is *after* this statement that Peter calls the people to a right response to their sin. Many times we excuse sin by citing our own ignorance, tiredness, inability to control ourselves, or by blaming our sin on the actions of others.

The right response to our sin is a changed heart and life. It is not enough to simply acknowledge our sin. It is not enough to say that we are sorry and move on.

We must walk away from lies and worthless things and instead offer right sacrifices. We must hate what is evil and cling to what is good. We must not remain in sin but remain in relationship with God.

Secondary Preaching Themes (based on 1 John 3:1-7)

As human beings, we identify ourselves in many different ways. We identify ourselves by our roles: student, boss, policeman, teacher, politician. We identify ourselves by our relationships: mother, brother, grandparent, friend. We identify ourselves by the groups we belong to. The way we identify ourselves affects how we react to the circumstances, pressures, opportunities, temptations, and frustrations we experience. In 1 John 3:1-7, we are reminded that we are called God's children. And John emphasizes that not only are we *called* God's children but that is our identity. That is who we are! Our identity comes from who God is and from him who is inextricably connected to God as our Father.

Our right response to sin flows out of our identity (1 John 3:1-7). We are God's children. We are made in his image. And one day we will be like him even more fully. As a result, we purify ourselves, seeking to be like God in the here and now. We are in relationship with the one who has no sin in him. And so we remain in this relationship, practicing righteousness, for that is our new and God-given identity.

Prayer of Repentance

Answer me when I cry out, my righteous God! Set me free from my troubles!

Have mercy on me! Listen to my prayer!

Answer me when I cry out, my righteous God! I acknowledge my wrongdoings. My sin is ever before me.

Have mercy on me, God, according to your faithful love! Wipe away my wrongdoings according to your great compassion!

Create a clean heart for me, God; put a new, faithful spirit deep inside me!

Please don't throw me out of your presence; please don't take your Holy Spirit away from me.

Return the joy of your salvation to me and sustain me with a willing spirit.

Benediction

May you neither ignore or excuse but may you respond rightly to your sin. With a changed heart and life, may you live out your true identity as a child of God. May you remain in right relationship with your Father God. And with your very being, may you preach a change of heart and life for the forgiveness of sins to all nations.

April 22, 2018

Passages: *Acts 4:5-12; Psalm 23; 1 John 3:16-24; John 10:11-18*

Gathering Prayer

O Lord, we gather in your name. In your name the sick become healthy. By the power of your name, our fears are dispelled. At the sound of your name, every knee will bow and every tongue will proclaim that you are Lord. In the name of Jesus, we are made right with God and washed clean. There is no other name under heaven by which we are saved. You have promised that where two or three gather in your name, you will be in our midst. We believe you. We acknowledge your presence with us. In Jesus's name, Amen.

Preaching Theme

Love is more than just words. Love is action. It is one thing to say, "I love you." It is another thing to live "I love you." And it is yet another thing altogether to die because of your love for someone else. In the words of 1 John 3:16a, "This is how we know love: Jesus laid down his life for us." We have been loved in the most profound and all-encompassing way imaginable. We matter to Jesus so much that he would sacrifice his own well-being over and over and eventually face death for our sakes.

While Jesus was crucified at the hands of the Romans and because of the nefarious intentions of the Jewish religious leaders, no one *took* Jesus's life from him. Rather, in John 10:18 Jesus tells us that he *willingly* laid down his own life. He died because he wanted to. He died, because he loves us so much.

How will we respond? First, will we allow ourselves to believe and to rely on the love Jesus offers us? Will we allow our hearts to know the reality that we are loved? We do not know love by watching love stories on TV. We do not know love by our own loved ones and how they treat us. We do not know love by listening to the thousands of love songs that have been written. Again, 1 John 3:16a says, "This is how we know love: Jesus laid down his life for us..."

But, the verse does not stop there. It continues: "...and we ought to lay down our lives for our brothers and sisters." Because we have been loved so completely and so extravagantly, will we offer this kind of love to those around us? Like Jesus, we can leave the comfort of our riches and our place of belonging and step into pain and displacement because of love. Like Jesus, we can leave our place at the table, take the posture of a servant, and do for others what they would rather not even do for themselves. Like Jesus, we can forfeit our own reputations by associating with people who are marginalized and condemned by society. Like Jesus, we can choose not to claim our own right but we can willingly sacrifice our rights so that others might know their worth.

Secondary Preaching Themes

The image of a shepherd is prevalent throughout scripture. Clearly in Psalm 23 and John 10 we see ourselves as sheep and the Lord himself as our shepherd. He cares for us in practical and eternal ways, giving his life for our well-being. What we cannot offer ourselves, he gives us. What we cannot do for ourselves, he does on our behalf. Because he is our Shepherd, we lack nothing.

There is power in a name. We can say famous names like Martin Luther King Jr., Mother Teresa, and Adolph Hitler and each elicits its own powerful response. After Peter and John had healed a lame man at the temple, the religious leaders were incensed and had only one question for them: "By what power or in what name did you do this?" (Acts 4:7). Boldly and unashamedly, Peter and John replied that it was in the name of Jesus Christ of Nazareth. They went on to say that Jesus's name is the only name under heaven by which people are saved. Because Jesus humbled himself and gave up his life on the cross, God the Father gave him the name above all names (Phil 2:8-9). And 1 John 3:23 declares that our response should be to "believe in the name of his Son, Jesus Christ, and love each other as he commanded us."

Offering Invitation

In view of God's mercy, we not only give our money today. In view of Jesus's sacrifice on our behalf, in these moments, we offer our lives. As we release our grasp on our riches, we also release our grasp on our own comfort, rights, privileges, and reputations.

Prayer of Repentance

We have gone astray like stubborn sheep, blindly following the lusts of our flesh and eyes. We confess that we are slow to learn how to avoid that which endangers our hearts. We are easily disoriented and confused. O Lord, guide us in proper paths for the sake of your good name.

We have refused rest and have busied ourselves at the expense of our own souls. We have taken pride in meaningless motion. We have justified our constant commotion. O Lord, lead us to still waters. Make us lie down. And restore our souls.

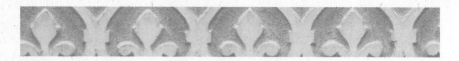

April 29, 2018

Passages: Acts 8:26-40; Psalm 22:25-31; 1 John 4:7-21; John 15:1-8

Call to Worship (from Psalm 22:25-26)

Leader: Why do you praise God today?

People: We offer praise in the great congregation because of who God is.

Leader: Why do you come to worship today?

People: We will fulfill our promises in the presence of those who honor God.

Leader: Let all those who are suffering eat and be full!

People: Let all who seek the Lord praise him!

All: May our hearts live forever.

Preaching Theme

The heart of our God is for people of every nation on this earth. He is the creator of the nations in the first place and he desires that the nations would rejoice and worship him. Psalm 86:9 declares that all the nations that God made will come and bow down before him and glorify his name. He has gone to great lengths to bless the nations through his people. In the scriptures, we see story after story of God using his people to cross cultural boundaries to bring his blessing to the ends of the earth. Through the witness of Naaman's servant girl, the wisdom of Joseph, and the counter-cultural posture of Jesus with the Samaritan woman at the well, God has been loving the nations.

In Acts 8:26-40, God inspires Philip to travel a desert road without giving him any clue as to why. Philip obeyed. God shows Philip an Ethiopian eunuch riding in a chariot on his way home from worshiping in Jerusalem. God commands Philip to approach the carriage and stay with it. Again, Philip obeys despite all the reasons he may have had to question such action. In the conversation that ensues, Philip starts with the Ethiopian man's questions and proclaims the good news about Jesus. Though the good news of Jesus's death and resurrection had occurred in Jerusalem, now it was on its way to Ethiopia because of God's love for the nations and the obedience of one disciple.

Psalm 22:27 says that "every part of the earth will remember and come back to the Lord; every family among all the nations will worship you." And verse 29 states, "Indeed, all the earth's powerful will worship him." Through an unlikely, yet divine encounter, the gospel made its way to the court of Queen Candace of Ethiopia through a eunuch who was the official responsible for her treasury.

Secondary Preaching Themes

There are so many delicious kinds of fruit. Apples, kiwis, pears, mangoes, African cherry oranges, pineapples, guava, blueberries, and the list goes on. Fruit trees and bushes seem to bear sweet and juicy fruit almost effortlessly. But the most beautiful apple tree branch has absolutely no hope of bearing fruit if it is disconnected from the tree. So it is with us. John 15:4 reminds us that we are completely unable to produce fruit unless we remain connected to Jesus. Verse 5 goes on to say that if we remain in him and he remains in us, we will produce much fruit.

In Acts 8:26-40, we see a beautiful example of a person connected to Jesus through the Holy Spirit. Philip simply obeyed the promptings of the Lord, letting the words of God dwell in him richly. And, as he did so, the fruit of repentance and baptism and life change and joy were borne in the heart of one Ethiopian man. But it didn't stop there. Tradition tells us that this one Ethiopian eunuch was sent into the regions of Ethiopia preaching the good news he had received and bearing much more fruit.

Prayer of Repentance

Father God, forgive us for the times we have not allowed ourselves to believe and receive your love for us. (Moment of silence.)

Son of God, forgive us for the times we have disconnected ourselves from you and tried to live life independently. (Moment of silence.)

Spirit of God, forgive us for the times you have prompted us and we have let our questions and excuses keep us from obeying you. (Moment of silence.)

Help us to remain in you. May your word remain in us. May your love remain in us. May you yourself remain in us.

Benediction

As you go out from here today, may you bear fruit because you are connected to Jesus himself. May you respond quickly and joyfully when the Holy Spirit prompts you. May you know and believe the love God has for you. And because God has loved you first, may you love others so that every family among all the nations will worship God. May God be glorified through us as we produce much fruit and prove that we follow Jesus our Lord. Amen.

May 6, 2018

Passages: Acts 10:44-48; Psalm 98; 1 John 5:1-6; John 15:9-17

Call to Worship

Leader: Shout triumphantly to the Lord, all the earth!

People: We shout triumphantly before the Lord, the king!

Leader: Sing your praises to the Lord with the sound of music.

People: With joy we will sing praise!

Leader: Let the sea and everything in it roar; the world and all its inhabitants too.

People: We lift our voices to exalt the one who is worthy!

Leader: Let all the rivers clap their hands; let the mountains rejoice out loud altogether.

People: God will establish justice in the world rightly; God will establish justice among all people fairly.

Preaching Theme

The story of Acts 10 is a story of shattered stereotypes. Peter's understanding of what was clean and unclean was dramatically challenged. It is a story of outsiders reaching out to insiders. The Gentile outsider, Cornelius, is prompted by God to initiate contact with the Jewish insider, Peter. It is a story of seeing beyond what we have known previously. The Jewish believers had never truly considered that Gentiles could know and follow Jesus. It is a story of how God's Spirit can touch and transform even those we would consider to be the most unusual suspects. Notice that verse 45 points out that the "believers who had come with Peter were astonished that the gift of the Holy Spirit had been poured out *even on the Gentiles.*"

All of us, if we are honest, have people who we think are unlikely candidates for God's grace. They may come from a different background than we do. They may speak a different language. They may follow a different religion. They may have done horrible, unspeakable things. They may seem to us to want nothing to do with Jesus. Their very existence may challenge our faith.

And so we do not share with them the good news of Jesus. We are afraid they might become argumentative or combative. We don't make flyers to invite them to our church. We are not sure we want them in our church. They are not our target audience. But, does our target audience match God's target audience? Are we willing to allow God to speak to us and open us up to the people he is drawing to himself no matter how unlikely they seem to us?

Be honest. Would you have chosen Peter with his head-strong nature and his tendency to swing from one extreme to the other? Would you have chosen Saul, a murderer of Christians, to be the first missionary and represent Jesus to people who had never heard of him before? Would you have considered an Ethiopian eunuch a worthy candidate to be an ambassador of the good news to an entire nation? Would you have chosen yourself, knowing your own fatal flaws and failures?

Secondary Preaching Themes

In John 15 and in 1 John 5, we see a connection between love and commands. History has shown us many examples of the kinds of leaders who issue commands and how unloving they can be. As a result, these two concepts can seem to be almost contradictory from our human perspective. But, the connection between them is strong in these two passages. If we keep Jesus's commandments, we remain in his love (John 15:10). Jesus has set the example for us of keeping the Father's commandments and remaining in his love (John 15:10). Jesus commands us to love one another as he has loved us (John 15:12). And, Jesus gives us his commands so that we might love one another (John 15:17). If we love God, we keep his commandments (1 John 5:3).

Prayer of Assurance

Thank you, Jesus, that your grace is broader than the scope of my sin.

Thank you, Jesus, that your grace goes deeper than my shame.

Thank you, Jesus, that your grace is sufficient in my weakness.

Thank you, Jesus, that your grace is stronger than my misconceptions and stereotypes.

Thank you, Jesus, that your grace reaches even the most defiled. Thank you, Jesus, that your grace reaches even me.

Benediction

Let us love the people God loves no matter how unlovely we think they are.

Let us love one another as we have been loved by Jesus.

Let us be willing to be surprised at how God's grace reaches the ones we would consider most unlikely or unworthy.

May we enjoy friendship with Jesus as we follow his commands.

May we revel in God's grace and proclaim God's mercy with joy.

Amen.

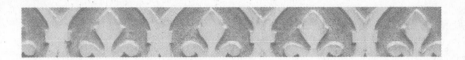

May 10, 2018–Ascension Day

Passages: Acts 1:1-11; Psalm 47 or 93; Ephesians 1:15-23; Luke 24:44-53

Call to Worship (based on Psalm 47)

Leader: Clap your hands, all you people! Shout joyfully to God!

People: Because the Lord Most High is awesome, he is the great king of the whole world.

Leader: Sing praise to God!

People: Sing praises to our king! Sing praises because God is king of the whole world!

Leader: God is king over the nations. God sits on his holy throne.

People: We are his people gathered, belonging to God; God is exalted beyond all.

Preaching Theme

For the forty days between his resurrection and ascension, Jesus spent time with his disciples teaching about the kingdom of God. Now that the disciples have "resurrection lenses"—or, given the oral tradition of Jesus's teaching methods, "resurrection ears"—Jesus repeats his teachings so that they may understand the ascension and what it means for the future. But even with Jesus working in the power of the Holy Spirit, the disciples have old worldviews that have yet to be overthrown. We see this in how they ask Jesus if *now* is the time that he's going to do the thing they have been waiting for him to do. They are still expecting a military messiah and the freedom of the nation of Israel. They may have "resurrection ears," but they do not have transformed "ascension minds" to understand that Jesus's ascension *is* his kingly rise and that this is good news for the whole world.

It will take the powerful presence and transforming work of the Holy Spirit within them to overthrow their worldview and propel them to heed Jesus's command to witness. We see this in how the Acts text ends. Jesus is lifted up out of their sight as the disciples continue to stare off into the sky, surely dumbfounded. Then two men in white appear and ask this odd question: "Why are you standing here, looking toward heaven? This Jesus, who was taken up from you into heaven, will come the same way that you saw him go into heaven" (Acts 1:11). Now, if Jesus will come back the same way he went, doesn't it actually make sense to keep looking for him to be lowered down from the sky? Not if you have an "ascension mind"! To know the power of resurrection and ascension is to understand that there is more than what meets the eye; that worldviews and presuppositions have to be shaken loose, and a new foundation has to be laid for the kingdom of God. The two men clothed in white are actually challenging the disciples: Will you do as Jesus—the ascended ruler of the whole world—commanded? It takes the work of the Holy Spirit through Jesus *and* in the life of every believer to give them "ascension minds" and kingdom lives.

Secondary Preaching Themes

Each of these texts' backbone is the power of God. In the Psalms, God's power is implied by God's total ability to subdue all the nations and gather all the peoples; God's worth and might is beyond all. Luke and Acts remind us that resurrection and ascension were accomplished by the same divine power source; according to Ephesians that same power is at work among God's people! Jesus's ministry is described by Luke in the opening verses of Acts as being "in the power of the Holy Spirit." Further, Jesus tells the disciples to wait until they've been "furnished with heavenly power" to fulfill their calling as witnesses. The bridge between what Jesus experienced and what we will experience is built by the powerful work of the Spirit.

There is a trinitarian focus to these New Testament passages as well. Jesus tells the disciples to wait for the gift that the Father has promised to them, which is the Holy Spirit. (The Spirit is not named in the Lukan account, but we know that the "power" Jesus is sending—and what the Father promised—is God the Spirit.) The prayer for the church in Ephesus describes the Father's will being accomplished by Jesus through the power (Holy Spirit) of God. This work is unshakeable, far above any kind of power we know here on earth, because this power is otherworldly; it is resurrection and ascension power. It is God.

Transition to Benediction

As Jesus was ascending to heaven, he lifted up his hands and offered a blessing upon his disciples. We are meant to remember that the same resurrected and ascended Savior blesses us each week through the raised hands and words of blessing that we now receive...

Sending (based on Ephesians 1:15-23)

Leader: You are empowered by the Spirit to see the revelation that God makes known to you.

People: We go with the eyes of our hearts to look for the hope of God's call and the richness of his inheritance for us.

Leader: You will find the overwhelming greatness of God's power at work!

People: We go with the powerful strength of God.

All: Amen!

May 13, 2018

Passages: Acts 1:15-17, 21-26; Psalm 1; 1 John 5:9-13; John 17:6-19

Preaching Theme

Character counts. In the Hebrew world, your name was a description of your character. Jesus prays for his disciples and draws upon the name, the character, of the Father over and over as he petitions for the welfare of his beloved...us.

Jesus is the character witness for the heavenly Father on earth. The character Christ reveals for the Father is one of loving protection and presence; because of God's character of love, we belong. Jesus revealed these truths in his testimony on earth, living the will of the triune God, and now, he prays for that work to continue in the name of the one who sent him. While the world may hate those whom Jesus loves, his love does not end with his time walking among them. Jesus asks that the Holy Father continue to watch over his children as he has always done because that is his loving character. It is the character that Jesus showed throughout his life and ministry because it was the name, the character, that the Father gave him to testify.

This prayer for safety is a prayer of someone who loves and trusts deeply. But we should expect nothing less from the God whose name and character is love. God is love and oh, how he loves us. How quick we are to forget. It is the loving character of God that keeps us safe from the evil one, gives us the life-giving word of God, bids us to receive God's holiness and truth. Jesus made himself holy for our sake, and makes us holy in the truth of God's character. Just as Jesus was sent into the world to share God's love, we go out spreading the character of Christ.

Secondary Preaching Themes

Theses texts provide pictures of receiving the testimony (word) of the Lord. Truly, it's a happy person who hears, receives, believes, and obeys (Ps 1). The reception of Jesus's revelation of the true character of God results in a crescendo of benefit for the believer in Jesus's prayer: protection, unity, purpose, holiness (John 17:6-19). The community that 1 John was written to was struggling to know which testimony to follow—that of the new teachers or that of the apostolic tradition? John tells them that God's testimony is always greater because it brings eternal life. To reject the word that has been passed down from the eyewitness apostles is to say that God is a liar (1 John 5:9-13). Finally, in Acts, the people trust God to actively testify to whom he wants to replace Judas as a disciple. After prayer for God's guidance, they cast the lots and don't question the result. Paramount to a life of faith is trust in the name of God and his loving character as revealed through his word.

Judas and his destruction provides a thought-provoking storyline in these texts. Is he the wicked who has sat with the disrespectful as they plot Jesus's arrest? Is he the one who stands in the road of sinners—literally the road walked to betray Christ? Is he the one who is destroyed like the dust that is blown away (Ps 1)? Might we see Judas's choice to hand Jesus over as an act of him choosing to believe human testimony of what's best for him (thirty pieces of silver) over God's testimony of self-sacrificing love (1 John 5:9-13)? But then again, Jesus's prayer in John 17 informs us that Judas's betrayal was done so that scripture would be fulfilled; this sentiment is repeated by the disciples when they announce the need to find Judas's replacement in Acts 1. Are these two storylines mutually exclusive? Was it because Judas could not accept the loving character and testimony of Christ that he became the one to fulfill the role of rejecting God?

Prayer of Repentance (based on Acts 1:24)

Lord, you know our deepest thoughts and desires. Show us which ones do not belong to your good will for us. In the silence, we listen for your pruning Spirit's work.

(Time of Silence)

We confess these things to you, O God, and pray that we find ourselves desiring and thinking of you and your kingdom above all else. In Jesus's name. Amen.

Commitment to Holy Living (Psalm 1)

Leader: Do you wish to be a happy person?

People: I do, God helping me.

Leader: And what has the Lord taught you about such things?

People: To love the Lord's instruction and think on it day and night.

Leader: And what will make you a happy person?

People: To be like a tree that bears fruit at just the right time in the name of Christ.

Sending (based on 1 John 5:9-13)

Leader: Go out with the testimony of Christ within you. Share with the world that God gave eternal life to you in word and deed.

People: This life is in the Son. This life is in us. We go out with God's great testimony for the world.

May 20, 2018–Pentecost Sunday

Passages: Acts 2:1-21 (or Ezekiel 37:1-4); Psalm 104:24-34, 35b;
Romans 8:22-27 (or Acts 2:1-21); John 15:26-27; 16:4b-15

Gathering Prayer (based on Acts 2:1-21)

*Our Lord and our God, we have gathered in this place together believing that it is your
Spirit who has drawn us here. We wait for your fierce presence. We trust that you, Holy
Spirit, are among us to enable us to speak your words in a world that so desperately needs
to hear them. Amen.*

Preaching Theme

The Spirit works to bring hope and life and the Spirit does it through us. The
spirit of the Lord drives Ezekiel into a desolate and dry valley full of even drier and
hopeless bones, the remnants of devastated people. The Spirit has Ezekiel prophesy
multiple times, delivering the message of God, calling upon the power of God to
do its promised work. God tells Ezekiel to proclaim the good news of life and hope
to a people who declare their own destitution and have given up. Ezekiel brings the
comforting presence of God to desperate places and people.

The spirit of God that we celebrate and call upon at Pentecost faithfully continues to do this work. In the beginning, the Spirit hovered over the chaos that was earth
and was breathed into dusty bones to make Adam come alive, who was then to be an
agent of God on earth. Throughout the time of the Old Testament, the spirit of God
spoke to key leaders and prophets about the will of God, the promises of God, and
the ways of life with God. When the exiled Israelites did not have hope, the Spirit
spoke through a prophet to comfort (at other times rebuking and chastising) and
remind them of God's promises. At the first Pentecost, the spirit of God came upon
the apostles and the first people to benefit were not the apostles themselves but those
gathered from every nation who were able to hear and understand the word of the
Lord as it was shared in their own language. Jesus calls the Holy Spirit our companion
and Paul says that the Spirit groans and prays for us to God. Even in these acts, we
see the call to be like the Spirit for others, comforting and walking alongside them
in troubling times, praying for them, sharing with them the promising work of God.

Ezekiel stands among a people in trouble, he prays to the breath of God to bring life, and he shares the promised work of God. He witnesses and is an agent of the Spirit.

Secondary Preaching Themes

Ezekiel 37:1-14 is about Yahweh bringing life to people by raising them up from their graves and putting his breath in them; Romans 8:22-27 is about the hope that God's people have for eternal life; and Psalm 104:29-30 declares that God gives and takes away the breath of life to all of creation. The spirit of God is the spirit of life.

One can see these texts sharing a theme of revealing God's plan or story. The vision in Ezekiel reveals God's desire to revive the hopeless people of Israel. Then, in Acts 2, we're told that many Jews (the people of Israel) from countries all over the "world" are living in Jerusalem and drawn into a crowd as they take interest in the work of the Holy Spirit among the apostles. Peter begins to preach to them and tells them that what they are witnessing is the continuation of God's plan of revival, this time quoting from the prophet Joel. If you choose to include Romans 8 in this week's texts, you can see how the story/God's plan has now taken on what God's revival has produced—namely, hope for eternity and the work of the Spirit here on earth. And in John 16 Jesus tells the disciples that the companion he and the Father are sending will only be continuing the work they have been doing, saying that the Spirit "won't speak on his own" and that "the Spirit takes what is mine and proclaims it to you" (vv. 13, 15).

Offering Invitation

Because of the work of the Holy Spirit among them, the apostles cause the crowd to be mystified, surprised, amazed, and bewildered. In our modern world, our sacrificial giving and sharing of resources through the offering is one of the ways we testify to the Spirit's work among us and cause others to be mystified and bewildered by our faith. May the Lord continue to do amazing things through these our gifts.

Introduction to Congregational Prayer (based on Romans 8:22-27)

We approach God in prayer with confidence and hope that whatever we pray, the Holy Spirit has come alongside of us to offer our prayers to the Father, offering his own prayers on our behalf, praying for God's perfect will to be done. Let us pray.

Benediction (based on Ezekiel 37:1-14)

The Lord raise you up from your graves of hopelessness and put his breath of life in you. May you live in the fertile land that God places you in, and know always that he is the Lord.

Groanings

Romans 8:18-25

Elisabeth DeVries

My friend Stacy went into labor with her second child while she was at home with her young daughter, Sophia. Her husband, Todd, was working so she was alone, playing with Sophia. The contractions began rather violently, causing her to double over in pain. Sensing that her pain and agony would probably scare little Sophia, Stacy stumbled her way into her bedroom and closed the door to call Todd. The conversation with Todd was short and to the point, something like, "Come home. Now!" followed by groaning through clenched teeth and shallow breathing. And after about a minute, Stacy composed herself, put on a smile, and returned to the living room to play with Sophia.

A few minutes later, feeling her stomach and back begin to tighten, she hurried her way back into the bedroom, shut the door, and rode out the contraction with her face in a pillow so that Sophia wouldn't hear her groaning in pain. She would do this with every contraction, so that little Sophia wouldn't be afraid. Because if a two-year-old sees her mother writhing and groaning in pain, a natural reaction is fear. We would expect little Sophia to run away scared. The little child doesn't understand what's going on; all she hears is her mother's scary groaning. Contrast that, though, with Todd's reaction to Stacy's groaning. Granted, there was probably a bit of fear...fear that he wouldn't get home in time to get her to the hospital. But hearing his wife on the phone, groaning with labor pains, was not primarily an occasion for fear. He gathered his things as quickly as he could and fumbled his keys in his hand as he ran out of his office, telling his coworkers, "It's finally happening! Stacy is having the baby!" Todd could interpret the groans with hope: something good was about to happen—the birth of his son.

In our text today, I imagine Paul writing this to the Roman Christians so that they would know how to interpret the groans they heard—the groans in creation and in their own hearts that pointed to the reality that things are not right, things are not as they're meant to be. Because there's a good chance that they were still like toddlers in their faith, unsure how to make sense of the groaning, hearing only pain and wanting to respond in fear. See, Paul has just written about the grace of life in the Spirit. "There is therefore no condemnation for those who are in Christ," Paul says (Rom 8:1, NRSV). "You are children of God. You are heirs of God and co-heirs with Christ," he says (see Rom 8:17). But we easily hear the objection because it has often been on our own lips: "But Paul, then what's with this deafening, horrifying groaning that floods our ears?" Things are not as they're meant to be.

We hear the groaning in creation. Things are not right. We hear the groaning of waves that are subjected to the futile task of continually dredging up our waste and placing it back at our feet on the seashore. After the *Deepwater Horizon* oil spill we heard creation groan as waves washed up some of the 130 million gallons of oil that were spilled. It came in the form of sticky brown balls, or fish that were belly up in brown sludge, or smothered turtles that washed up on shore. And frankly, depending on how much we care about wildlife and depending on how much of a connection we felt to the Gulf region, we may have heard this groaning as only mildly disturbing—unfortunate, but incidental. But five years later we heard the waves groan again as they washed up the little body of Aylan Kurdi, the Syrian refugee boy whose flimsy boat capsized en route to Greece. The moment was captured in a photograph, and the world looked on in horror. The groaning of the waves became deafening, horrifying. Things are not right; things are not as they're meant to be.

We hear the groaning in creation, and our hearts also groan under the weight of our present sufferings. See we're stuck in this in-between time; God's promises for salvation for his people have been set in motion through the birth, death, resurrection, and ascension of Jesus. But still, we wait for the final culmination of God's promises; we wait for the day when heaven and earth will meet, when there will be no more death or mourning or crying or pain. We wait for the day when God will renew all things; we wait for our future glory. And while we wait, our hearts groan—things are not as they're meant to be.

In the marriage counseling book *Getting the Love You Want*, the author describes a married couple whose hearts groaned under the weight of their marriage that was falling apart. They used to be so in love, but now they had grown apart, and the daily silence between them was deafening. And so this counselor gave them homework to work on sparking their connection again—they were told to spend one day together doing something they love to do. So one Saturday they set out to complete their assignment; they would go for a hike together, and then have dinner at a nice restaurant. At the last minute the wife remembered that their friend really wanted to check out this national park where they were going to hike, so they decided to bring him along. In the car on the way there the men sat up front and talked together while she sat quietly in the back, scrolling through her phone. Then on the hike the couple took turns walking next to him, asking about his job and talking about mutual friends. Maybe they would connect at dinner. But then they got to the restaurant and there was a jazz band playing so the husband suggested that they sit near the band so they could enjoy the music. They got home from their date that day, and after spending the whole day together they had still not connected. And so out of habit they turned on their favorite TV show and retreated back into their own heads...hearts still groaning as the cool silence took its place between them.

And of course there are a host of other things that make our hearts groan: broken friendships, a bad diagnosis from the doctor, infertility, the loss of a job, or the death of a loved one. The groaning becomes deafening, horrifying at times. And like small children, we don't really know what to do with the groaning—we don't know how to interpret it. We'd like to run away, hide, pretend as if everything is still okay—like if we ignore it then maybe it will go away.

But as Paul writes, he helps us to interpret the groaning—he helps us to change our perspective from frightened toddlers to expectant, mature believers. Paul suggests to us that when we hear creation groaning it is not the sound of creation giving up and surrendering to death or chaos. Rather, the groaning we hear is in expectation, eager expectation, as in the pains of childbirth. So the groaning is not an occasion to be afraid; rather it points us to the future. Something good is coming. God will put all things right.

Creation groans in hope. It is hoping for a time when God will reveal the full glory of his children and when God will liberate creation from its frustration. Creation is hoping for a time when the waves won't groan carrying the weight of spilled oil and young children but when they will be free to majestically break over rocky cliffs as God's children look on in awe and wonder. Creation groans because something good is coming. God will put things right.

So, too, Paul helps us to see that the achiness of our groaning hearts is not to be taken as a sign that chaos and evil have sabotaged God's good promises. Rather, the groaning we hear in ourselves is in eager expectation: expectation for the day when God will reveal his glory in us, when our adoption will be finalized, when God will redeem our bodies. So when our hearts groan, it is not an occasion for fear. Rather, it points us to the future. Something good is coming. God will put things right. We groan in hope.

But this is not a baseless hope, or a kind of naïve optimism. It is a hope that is founded on God's good gift of the Holy Spirit. When we don't know how to interpret the groaning that we hear and experience, it is the presence of the Holy Spirit that assures us something good is coming and things will be put right. A little kick from the baby in the midst of birth pains is an assurance for the groaning mother that something good is coming. So, too, the Holy Spirit in us is an assurance that God's plan for the liberation of creation and our future glory is still on track. The Holy Spirit in us is, in fact, the beginning of that good that is to come. In the Holy Spirit God has already begun to put things right. And so we groan in hope.

In the wake of the Paris attacks in November 2015 and then the ensuing debates about refugees, the groaning grew to a deafening roar . . . things are not as they're supposed to be. And it was awfully easy to feel fear rather than hope, wasn't it? Terrorism has a way of doing that, I suppose. But in those troubling days I ran across a video from the Christian non-profit organization Samaritan's Purse—and it was an assurance for me that God is indeed at work, that something good is coming. This video tells about volunteers working on the islands of Greece with the floods of refugees arriving on the shores. It shows young men, old women, children, and their parents all crammed onto a rickety boat, being tossed around by the waves.

But on shore the volunteers look through binoculars, anticipating where the boat will meet the shore, anticipating where they must run to meet these cold, wet, desperate refugees. Volunteers run to meet the boat and they're handed small shivering children. They take off the children's wet clothes and quickly cover them with space blankets and hold them close to warm them up. One of the volunteers, Hannah, says, "A lot of the moms are very visibly afraid and to be handed someone else's child is very humbling . . . to be responsible, to care for them even for that brief moment."[1] While governments fortify their borders and countless people bicker on social media about the myriad of things *we'd* like to do with the refugees, God's Spirit interpreted the groaning for these Christians and moved them to respond to this refugee crisis in hope. The fact that they are able to act without fear for their own safety and to show love indiscriminately to refugees of all ages and faiths and genders is evidence of that hope. It's the hope that something good is coming. It's hope that God will put all things right, that he has already begun, and he has invited us to join him.

And sisters and brothers, as the Holy Spirit lives in us, he interprets the groaning that we hear and feel and points us to the future. He gives us hope and emboldens us to embody that hope that is ours and bring it to a world that is eagerly waiting for the days of Revelation 21: when God will dwell among his people again, when he will wipe away every tear from their eyes, when there will be no more death or mourning or crying or pain. So when we hear the groaning we know: a good thing is coming. God will put all things right. In fact, he has already begun to put things right by the power of the Holy Spirit, and he has invited us to join him. Thanks be to God.

May 27, 2018–Trinity Sunday

Passages: Isaiah 6:1-8; Psalm 29; Romans 8:12-17; John 3:1-17

Call to Worship (based on Psalm 29)

Leader: You divine beings! Give to the Lord glory and power!

People: We give to the Lord the glory due his name!

Leader: Bow down to the Lord in holy splendor!

People: The Lord sits enthroned; he is king forever!

Leader: Let the Lord give strength to his people!

People: Let the Lord bless us with peace!

Preaching Theme

Belonging to the family of God directs the character of our lives. Most of us grew up knowing key family values: things like never showing weakness in public, excelling in academics or sports, caring for those who could not care for themselves, and so forth. These guiding principles helped us know how to live and relate to the world. They reminded us of who we were and how we ought to be. Sometimes, we failed to live by them and depending on how important these things were to our family, we ran the risk of losing our belonging. For some, we even stood the chance of losing our inheritance.

Paul uses similar language about being family, of being shaped by guiding principles from outside of our own will, and of understanding that our lives speak to the character of the one to whom we belong. In the case of the family made by Christ through the Spirit, though, our inheritance is never at stake: it is God's gift to us and is totally separate from anything we do. What people should see in us is how close to the Spirit we are, how much we have followed the Spirit's guidance and knowledge in our hearts and minds, as God's adopted children. If we are children of the king, then our lives are meant to reflect God's kingdom values! If we are heirs of God's kingdom, then our lives will be spent making that kingdom a beautiful place full of God's Spirit.

Secondary Preaching Themes

The Lord is a mighty king with a mighty voice. Psalm 29 lists all of the majestic things that the king's voice can do on earth. God's voice thunders over the waters (vibrating it); breaks and shatters cedars; makes nations frolic like young and wild animals; the Lord's voice shakes the wilderness and convulses the oak trees, stripping the bark off of the forest's trees. Who else can do such things by only the use of their voice? Isaiah 6:1-8 gives us a more intimate picture of the mighty king's heavenly throne room. Instead of God's voice, it's the shouts of worship from the winged creatures surrounding the Lord that profoundly impact Isaiah. Isaiah says that they are shouting; might they be shouting because the voice of the Lord—and all that it does on earth—is so loud that they must shout to be heard? Their shouts of praise shake the doorframe and lead Isaiah to repent of the misuse of his own voice (lips). God does miraculous and awe-inspiring things with his voice; the voices of those in the throne room offer praise; and God sends others into the world to use their voice to share his message.

Another connection between a number of these texts is how we respond to God's invitation. Isaiah answers it when he says to God, "I'm here; send me." Paul teaches it in Romans when he urges followers of Christ to be led by God's Spirit, since we have received "a Spirit that shows [we] are adopted as [God's] children." The opposite of accepting this as our way of life is to continue to live "on the basis of selfishness," ultimately rejecting the Spirit's invitation to see ourselves as heir of the king. Finally, Nicodemus shows a desire to respond to God's invitation in that he sought out Jesus in the night, but the story moves on before we're told what Nicodemus decided to do. Nicodemus asked to have things explained to him, but he didn't respond in any way to what Jesus teaches him about being born of the Spirit.

Call to Confession (based on Isaiah 6:1-8)

When confronted with the holy worship of God in his throne room, Isaiah's first response is confession. "I'm a man with unclean lips, and I live among a people with unclean lips." Having joined in the heavenly worship of God, we turn now, as Isaiah did, to a time of confession.

Assurance of Pardon (based on John 3:1-17)

Believe these words of truth: "God so loved the world that he gave his only Son, so that everyone who believes in him won't perish but will have eternal life. God didn't send his Son into the world to judge the world, but that the world might be saved through him."

Sending (based on Isaiah 6:1-8)

Leader: The Lord God asks, "Whom should I send, who will go for us" to share what we have heard and seen here today?

People: "Here I am, send me."

Leader: Go out with the power of the Spirit to complete all that Christ sets before you.

June 3, 2018

Passages: 1 Samuel 3:1-10 (11-20); Psalm 81:1-10; 2 Corinthians 4:5-12;
Mark 2:23–3:6

Call to Worship (from Psalm 81)

As we gather in the name of our risen Savior, Jesus Christ, we shout to the God our strength, we sing and strike up the music to give praise to the God of our salvation. God has led us out of the slavery of sin. Let us praise God with glad voices!

Preaching Theme

Nestled as it is with these other lectionary passages, Mark 2–3 reflect a kind of sad poignancy. It's the Sabbath once again, but it seems in the Gospels that this "festive day of rest" is seldom festive and not terribly restful for anyone. The Sabbath instead becomes the abiding flashpoint between Jesus and his critics. Jesus alone incarnates God's full intention for this restorative day that celebrates both creation and redemption, but whenever he tries to bring that word of God to the Pharisees, he gets at best ignored and at worst actively ganged up on.

What a contrast this provides to the boy Samuel. The word of God, we are told, was pretty rare at that time. Israel and its leaders had fallen away from covenant faithfulness. But then God comes to the young man only to find a receptive vessel for his word and for his truth. It was a hard thing Samuel had to hear—and an even harder truth to tell to hapless old Eli—but the one whose name means "God hears" in turns hears God and, not for the last time in his life, follows what he hears. Speaking of receptive vessels, Paul's famous image in 2 Corinthians 4 of simple clay pots likewise shows the tender side of God's revelation to us. God entrusts the very gospel to people who are as frail as they are flawed. Yet somehow the humble simplicity of such earthen vessels itself matches the humble Savior who is at the center of that good news.

The Pharisees have no such tender receptivity when it comes to encountering the living Word of God, the Word both enfleshed by Jesus and spoken from his very lips. It's clear in Mark 3 that Jesus has been set up. A man with a withered hand is strategically placed inside the synagogue where the Pharisees know Jesus will run across him. They sit back and watch. When challenged by a question from Jesus, they stay as silent as the grave, or, better said, as the whitewashed sepulchers they are. Jesus leans into the real purpose of the Sabbath by restoring a fractured piece of creation. But there is not a hint of rejoicing. No one praises God or breaks into song. And the reason is simple: they had become impervious to the Word. They were not open and receptive like a child. They were not simple vessels waiting to be filled. They were not, to use the image in Psalm 81:10, like hungry baby birds who opened their mouths to be filled with good things from God. No, they were arrogant steel traps, sealed off from God's truth.

Of course, we all hope we're more like Samuel and jars of clay than this. And maybe most of the time we are. Still, we all know how we, too, can become quickly resistant the moment we sense God's word is challenging us or some longstanding practice in our lives or some deeply entrenched belief. It's an ongoing challenge in the Christian life to say again and again with Samuel, "Speak. Your servant is listening."

Secondary Preaching Themes (Psalm 81)

It's a shame the lectionary would have us stop reading this poem at the tenth verse. True, verse 11 begins sharper language of judgment, and it seems sometimes the lectionary folks would spare us such unhappiness. But the truth is we need these words of judgment and lament against Israel because sometimes they need to be spoken over us as well. And it's properly sobering and clarifying to recognize that truth.

But it's not just because of the words of judgment that we need the last part of Psalm 81. It's also because of all the grace that gets mingled into those harsher sentiments. God won't relent or be put off quite so easily. Yes, he was angry with his people. Yes, he turned them over to their enemies on account of wholesale covenant failure. But even then God had the "if only" longing we see again and again in even some of the harshest of Old Testament judgment texts. If only the people came back, God would be right there, still ready to fill their mouths with good things. It's a reminder of the insight of the great Jewish theologian Abraham Heschel: the God of Israel is never fundamentally an angry God. Never. He is always loving and the fullness of that love is forever available at a moment's notice!

Blessing (from 2 Corinthians 4)

May the God who let the light shine out of darkness shine in also your hearts and minds to fill you with the splendor of his grace and love.

June 10, 2018

*Passages: 1 Samuel 8:4-11 (20-25); Psalm 130; 2 Corinthians 4:13–5:1;
Mark 3:20-35*

Gathering Prayer

Almighty God of grace and mercy, we, your people, are gathered to be in your presence, to give ourselves to you anew. Some of our paths have been rough with trials, misunderstandings, and we have felt overwhelmed by what is happening in the world. But our eyes are on you! Our hopeful hearts kneel before you with awe! We are in harmony as one body, remembering the many victories that you have won for us in our lives and our world! Receive our adoration for you as we free our minds to worship only you. In the name of our true Lord and Savior, Jesus Christ, we pray. Amen.

Preaching Theme

When the Israelite elders came to Samuel and asked him to appoint a new king for them, he had to have been heartbroken. Samuel was getting old. The elders did not believe that his sons were fit to succeed him. It was apparent that the Israelites had not only forgotten where they came from, but who brought them out of their slavery to the Egyptians. After hundreds of years of crying out to God, this people seemed to have forgotten the one who not only answered their prayers, but the only king who has the supernatural power *to answer them.*

The elders wanted a human king like all the other nations. They wanted a king who had strong leadership attributes, but one whom they could see, hear, and touch without a prophet who served as a liaison between them and a Sovereign whose ways they did not comprehend.

Like many of us today, however, the Israelites were not willing to be led by God while they waited for the King of kings whom God promised. Through the miracles, signs, and wonders that God had shown them throughout their liberation from multigenerational oppression, the Lord more than proved that he had all the attributes they were seeking in a leader. Yet even after Samuel delivered the message describing their next king, they were willing to submit themselves to mistreatment again for the sake of "knowing right now" rather than waiting under God's provision until his chosen Ruler took the throne. Too often, we are willing to settle for what we can see and understand, rather than wait and trust God for his best. In the settling, we reject the full manifestation of God's goodness in our lives.

Secondary Preaching Themes

2 Corinthians 4:13–5:1

It is often difficult to be patient while we wait for a change in circumstance to come when our minds are focused on what is right in front of us. Waiting on and with God can be difficult while enduring challenges with family members, health problems, or simply the day-to-day business of navigating life.

It is beneficial for Christ followers to daily and intentionally remember what the Apostle Paul wrote to the church at Corinth in 2 Corinthians 4:15: "All these things are for your benefit. As grace increases to benefit more and more people, it will cause gratitude to increase, which results in God's glory."

Remembering the acts of grace that God extends to us every day (yes, *every* day) increases our gratitude toward him. Facing a dilemma while recalling that God either got us out of a similar situation or kept us sane while he brought us through a worse situation brings peace and, eventually, patience.

Practicing being grateful makes the waiting with God easier to bear.

Mark 3:20-35

One of the risks of serving a human leader is the possibility of control. Human flaws create the opening for leaders to be controlled and manipulated by those whom they serve and vice versa. It is for this reason that it is critically important to serve under the governance of Jesus Christ, whether leader or follower.

The term *power* is a constant in everyday language. We talk about power in the contexts of business, government, even the church. As the Gospel of Mark reminds us, however, only Jesus Christ has true power. Through Jesus, we have the gift of forgiveness of sins. This is something no human being has the power to do.

Responsive Reading (based on Psalm 130)

Leader: We hope, Lord.

People: Our whole being hopes, and we will wait for God's promise.

Leader: Our whole being waits for the Lord—more than the night waits for morning;

People: Yes, more than the night watch waits for the morning!

Leader: Yes, we will wait for the Lord!

People: Faithful love is with the Lord; because great redemption is with our God!

All: God is the one who will redeem us from all our sin!

Benediction

As we leave this place, we thank you, Lord, that you are sending us out into the world as a people who are led by the King of kings and the Lord of lords. We invite you to teach us how to wait with you, remembering what you have done in the past, knowing that you will give us your best for the present and the future. In Jesus's name we pray. Thank you!

June 17, 2018

Passages: *1 Samuel 15:34–16:13; Psalm 92:1-4, 12-15; 2 Corinthians 5:6-10 (11-13), 14-17; Mark 4:26-34*

Call to Worship (based on Psalm 92:1-4)

People: It is good to give thanks to the Lord,

Leader: To sing praises to your name, Most High

People: To proclaim your loyal love in the morning, your faithfulness at nighttime

Leader: With the ten-stringed harp, with the melody of the lyre

People: Because you've made me happy, Lord, by your acts

All: We sing with joy because of your handiwork.

Preaching Theme

Samuel is still grieving because God has rejected King Saul, the people's king. The prophet's grief does not deter God from giving him another assignment—to anoint the new king, God's choice ruler.

Although Samuel has been in constant communication with the Lord his entire life, here his fear causes him to question God's instructions. In 1 Samuel 15:2, the servant is more afraid of Saul than he is of the one who created him. No matter how mature we may feel we are in our growth in the Christ-following lifestyle, there are times when our emotions will cause us to find the sovereign God impractical. The example that Samuel sets for us in this story encourages us to continue the dialogue rather than end it with unproductive perceptions. Faith will indeed spring up.

Samuel, ready to anoint Saul's successor, meets all of Jesse's sons. The prophet anticipated one tall, rugged young man after the other as God's special leader. Yet none of them, in spite of how Samuel might have imagined a king (perhaps a man who was tall, resembling Saul), made the cut. But there was one son left. In 1 Samuel 16:11, Samuel tells the boy's father, "Send for him . . . because we can't proceed until he gets here." No one in the house was going to have dinner until the youngest boy returned.

David spent most of his time out in the pasture tending to the sheep. How fitting that he was an ancestor of the Good Shepherd, Jesus! David was the smallest, the youngest of all his brothers. Yet everyone present had to wait for his return home from the fields before Samuel could complete his task.

Being a shepherd can be very lonely, yet David kept company not only with his flock but with the Lord. Undoubtedly, he spent many hours of every day enjoying conversations with God. Unlike his predecessor, David was so comfortable conversing with his Lord that throughout his career as the leader of Israel, he did very little without consulting God before making decisions that impacted his people.

Neither Samuel nor his family believed he was a likely candidate. God selected the person who had a heart for him. God selected someone who knew him so well that he had confidence in his goodness and wisdom. David was a king worth waiting for.

Secondary Preaching Themes

2 Corinthians 5:6-10 (11-13), 14-17

In order for our hearts to be shaped, molded, and ultimately changed so that we become who God wants us to be, we must be in relationship with him. That often means following Jesus into territories without having any idea what the outcomes will be. Like a GPS for an automobile, we may enter the correct address, but if there is unanticipated road work, the voice in the machine may tell us that it has to recalculate and guide us to our destination by another route. By faith, we expect to get to our location. By faith in the Lord, we also expect to get there safely, even if the roads are unfamiliar.

The faith we exercise grows over time, with a Christ-consciousness that teaches us to pay attention to the spiritual as well as the obvious. We learn to tell the difference when we understand, as the Apostle Paul wrote in 2 Corinthians 5:7-8, "We live by faith and not by sight. We are confident..."

Mark 4:26-34

In the Gospel of Mark, Jesus tells a parable about the mustard seed, the smallest seed on earth. When eating a hot dog with mustard, very few of us pause before the first bite to consider the origin of the condiment that makes our food taste better.

As Jesus describes the mustard seed, it begins small and has great impact on the earth. The tree branches are widespread and provide space for birds' nests. The mustard seed, when planted, is not impacted by its surroundings, but it has great impact on its surroundings. God uses what humankind perceives to be small or insignificant to impact the world. It is his love and empowerment that makes what is great, great.

Prayer of Application

Dear heavenly Father, we are so grateful that you invite us to know you more. Open our eyes so that we see the obvious and the unseen. Help us to enjoy conversation with you until we are so confident in you, our faith gives us the courage to follow you without pause. In Christ's name we pray. Amen.

Benediction

By your Holy Spirit, empower us to advance your kingdom, O God, spreading your love and sharing your word like the branches of a mustard tree. In Jesus's name we pray. Amen.

June 24, 2018

*Passages: 1 Samuel 17: (1a, 4-11, 19-23) 32-49; Psalm 107:1-3, 23-32;
2 Corinthians 6:1-13; Mark 4:35-41*

Gathering Prayer

Almighty God, the Lord of Hosts, you are welcome in this place and in our lives. As we center ourselves, prepare our hearts to be filled with your Holy Spirit. We offer you our praise because you are worthy. We want more of you, God, so we worship you. In Jesus's name we pray.

Preaching Theme

The story of the battle between young David and Goliath the giant is one of the best-known stories in the Bible. Movies have been made about this story. Children's books and television shows have retold this wonderful drama about the boy who defeated the threatening man with a sling shot and five smooth stones. What a great ending! Who doesn't love to see the underdog win at the end?

Clearly, this is more than a children's story. God once again shows us who he is, even though he seems to be silent. We not only find young David testifying about his confidence in the heavenly Father who saved him and his flock from lions and bears, but we see how God empowers a little warrior to do the impossible. David showed up and trusted what he knew about God as a result of his own experience with him. In return, the Lord gave him the victory in the face of those who doubted him.

David also teaches us about authenticity. Too often we think that we cannot serve the Lord unless or until we fit into an invisible mold that makes us fit some image of worthiness (that really doesn't exist). In Ephesians 6:10-17, the Apostle Paul instructs believers to put on the whole armor of God. This spiritual armor is not one size fits all. It is armor that fits every size. It is just as powerful on a petite body as it is a tall and large body. And the best armor is the tried armor.

First Samuel 17:38-40 describes how Saul dressed David in his armor. David told Saul, "I can't walk in this because I've never tried it before." So he removed it and took up his staff. We know what happened next.

David spent a lot of time with the Lord. He was not only comfortable in his own skin, but he was comfortable as he was in God's presence. Saul's royal battle fatigues were unnecessary. David was clothed in the righteousness of Christ. His relationship with the Lord was the comfortable, tried attire that gave him the freedom and power to take down Goliath.

Secondary Preaching Themes

Psalm 107

Psalm 107 and the text from the Gospel of Mark talk about storms disturbing the seas. A storm is a common metaphor for difficulties that emerge in the course of life. Storms are often unexpected. Although we can enjoy the most sound, peaceful sleep during a good thunderstorm (as Jesus demonstrated in Mark), they can be disruptive, sometimes dangerous.

Whether a literal or metaphorical storm, God has the power to speak to it. By the power delegated to believers by Jesus Christ, the Holy Spirit can give us the wisdom to see the beginnings of a storm like a misunderstanding in a relationship, a health challenge, or another distracting circumstance and tell us how to dismantle it before it has a chance to manifest.

When we choose to follow Jesus and live into God's word, even when we don't see the storm on the horizon, he will protect us through the storm. We need to show up as we are, believing in the knowledge we gain from knowing God and standing in faith.

2 Corinthians 6:1-13

Serving the Lord is not easy. Ministers—whether clergy or laity—are faced with many challenges while living to advance God's kingdom on earth. Opposition, lack of understanding, financial problems, persecution are often part of the journey. But it is worth it all because we love the Lord. His people are blessed in many ways when we live for him.

The Apostle Paul shares a little about this in 2 Corinthians. Many are the battles that he and his ministers endure and live to tell about. The Holy Spirit within them gave them the strength to endure and help them grow in faith as they continued to share the good news of Jesus Christ.

Prayer of Gratitude

Thank you, God, for the many battles—seen and unseen—that you have fought for us. Thank you for speaking peace to the storms that could have overtaken us. Thank you for defeating the giants that have tried to destroy us. Now we offer ourselves to you, grateful for who you are. In Jesus's mighty and precious name we pray. Amen.

Sending Forth

When we leave this place, we embark on a new beginning. God is opening doors for us to joyfully share what we know about him through his Son and Holy Spirit. Know that you can do all things, endure all things through Jesus Christ. Go in authenticity, honesty, and love. Go in strength. Go in Jesus's name. Amen.

July 1, 2018

Passages: 2 Samuel 1:1, 17-27; Psalm 30; 2 Corinthians 8:7-15; Mark 5:21-43

Call to Worship (based on Psalm 30)

Leader: We exalt you, Lord, because you pulled us up

People: You didn't let our enemies celebrate over us

Leader: Lord, we cried out to you for help

People: And you healed us.

Leader: Lord, you brought us from a dark place,

People: You brought us back to light and life.

Leader: Lord, help us to be faithful to you.

People: We will sing praises to you

Leader: Weeping may stay all night, but joy will come in the morning!

All: We give thanks to his holy name. Morning joy will surely come!

Preaching Theme

David has grown up. He was a faithful soldier in King Saul's army. God preserved him through many wars, Saul's jealousy, attempts on his life, and the complexities of a dysfunctional family that fiercely loved him. Through war, David loses his king and his best friend. He will soon have to assume the throne.

In 2 Samuel 1 David learns of the death of his king and father-in-law, Saul. He also learns of the death of Jonathan, his friend and brother-in-law. While grieving, David must also accept that his life is about to change even more dramatically than it had in the past. He has lost a friend and an enemy; he has gained a kingdom and freedom from the wrath of his predecessor.

God's chosen ruler could have responded in a number of ways, but he chose to affect the closure of those relationships by honoring the fallen in a somewhat ironic manner.

In verses 19-27, David sings a hymn in honor of Saul and Jonathan with the refrain, "Look how the mighty warriors have fallen!" The great soldiers are eulogized, yet decried for the blood they shed. David mourns their fall and exalts the love he and the people of Israel had for them.

David approached the end of an era that could have killed him through no fault of his own by ending on a high road. He publicly mourned the loss of a royal regime by honoring their legacy. When one leg of a life's journey ends, we can face the next leg with faith when we choose to lift up the good that should be remembered and put away bitter language.

Secondary Preaching Themes

Mark 5:21-43

In order for the woman in the crowd to be healed by Jesus, he had to lose some of his virtue. The woman had to put aside all timidity and fear in order to touch his garment in the presence of so many witnesses. Desperation and faith were required for her to be made whole.

There are times when it is necessary for us to give up or lose something in order for our lives to change for the better. In this passage, Jesus lost palpable energy and gave up his right to punish this woman for touching him.

David lost persons who were dear to him before he could live into his destiny. The woman in the crowd faced the possibility of losing her freedom in order for her to become healthy. Jesus lost his life in order for us to receive the gifts of salvation and physical and spiritual healing.

2 Corinthians 8:7-15

When a person first accepts Jesus Christ as their Savior and invites him to be Lord in their life, most often, they are so excited and enthusiastic, they are almost giddy with joy. The new believer wants to read, hear, experience everything they can so that they may take in more of God.

Over time, especially as nonbelievers and the adversary try to shake their faith, the enthusiasm begins to die down, if not die out. The Apostle Paul reminds the church at Corinth that they don't have to live out their faith until it dies. He encourages them to live into the gift grace that we have in God. The passionate love that they had when they first came to know Christ should not diminish over time. Their loving service to the Lord could and should be as exuberant and committed at the end of their journey as it was in the beginning.

Prayer of Repentance

Loving and merciful God, we confess that there were times when we preferred to recall bitter memories instead of celebrating the victories you sent our way. We repent for acting out of hurt instead of faith. We repent that we have at times allowed ourselves to be distracted by our troubles instead of redirecting our thoughts to grateful remembrances. Please forgive us, Lord. In the name of Jesus Christ we pray. Amen.

Benediction

May the God of New Beginnings bless each of us with the fire of love for him and all creation. As we attempt to win our communities for Jesus Christ, let us speak life. Let us celebrate God's good works. Let us honor him, his servants, and all whom he loves. In the Savior's name we pray. Amen.

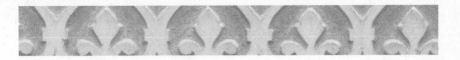

July 8, 2018

Passages: *2 Samuel 5:1-5, 9-10; Psalm 123; 2 Corinthians 12:2-10; Mark 6:1-13*

Gathering Prayer

O God, we gather this morning in your love and grace. Reveal to us deeper truths about our condition, that we might renew our commitment to your way. Amen.

Preaching Theme

The story of Jesus's rejection in his own hometown is well documented among the Gospel writers. Matthew, Mark, and Luke all talk about it. John and the non-canonical Gospel of Thomas both share the quote "No prophet is accepted in his own village."

But Mark's version is unique in this way: in chapter 6 verse 5, after the people rejected him, Jesus was "*unable* to do any miracles there, except that he placed his hands on a few sick people and healed them." Matthew softens the language in his version, saying that Jesus simply *did not do* any miracles, indicating that Jesus could if he wanted to, but chose otherwise.

There is no mistaking what Mark is suggesting here. Jesus's power to heal is contingent on one's willingness to believe.

That might seem like an awfully troubling notion at first. Many prefer to believe in a God who is omnipotent, a God who can do anything, a Jesus who can heal anyone, a Lord who can redeem even the most wayward soul. Good Protestant Christians hate to put any contingencies on God's gracious activity, and if for even a moment we say that the effectiveness of God's grace depends on our willingness to accept it, then our acceptance becomes a work that is necessary for salvation. At the very least, we come up with bumper sticker–sized half-truths such as "God helps those who help themselves." It is easy for us to quickly spin out the troubling implications of Mark 6:5.

So what do we do? Well, Mark gives us a hint with what happens next. Whereas Matthew next talks about the death of John the Baptist, and both Luke and John move Jesus and his disciples to Galilee, Mark tells a different story. It is here that Jesus sends the disciples out on a mission, two by two, into the surrounding villages. He instructs them to go out without money or bags, and nothing but the staff in their hand and the sandals on their feet.

In other words, Jesus moves into pursuit mode. He shifts his mission into an aggressive campaign to go out to where the people are, to lure them, woo them, and give them the opportunity to experience God's power.

In theological terms, and particularly in terms of Wesleyan theology, Jesus demonstrates prevenient grace. It is the grace afforded to all of humanity that operates in our lives before we are able to recognize it. It enables us to accept God's grace and profess our faith in Jesus Christ, so that our act of acceptance is not a work needed to *earn* God's grace, but is only possible *because* of God's grace.

Ultimately, Mark, more than the other Gospels, allows for an affirmation of human free will. But he is careful to couple this notion with a depiction of God's love that will not let us go, and will go to great lengths to enable us to say yes to Jesus.

Secondary Preaching Themes

In a way, Paul's letter to the Corinthians is the *opposite* of the Mark story. Paul's problem was not that he lacked belief and therefore could not be healed; he fully believed that God could heal him, even entreating God to do so on three different occasions, yet he perceived that God would not.

As troubling as it may be to consider a God with limited power, it is equally troubling to think about a God of limited love. Yet, these two passages together, Mark and Corinthians, form the basis of the classic dilemma of theodicy: If God is all-loving and all-powerful, then why is there suffering and evil in the world? One must either change one's perception of God's omnipotence (which Mark in some way attempts to do) or alter one's definition of God's love.

This is Paul's conclusion. It is not that God wants Paul to suffer, but God is allowing Paul to suffer in order to strengthen Paul's resolve, and so that God's power can be perfected in Paul's weakness.

In laying out the theodicy problem using these two texts, the preacher may choose to allow space for people in the congregation to wrestle through these conclusions for themselves: "What is it that I believe about God in the midst of my suffering? Do I believe that God is empowering me to do something about it, or is God using this suffering to demonstrate God's power and love?"

Prayer of Application

O God, we thank you that you draw near to us in Jesus, and through him we have the means to connect with you deeply and intimately. You sense the nature of our suffering, and choose to join us in the midst of it.

May the promise of Paul become true to us. As your grace is sufficient to our need, may your power be made perfect in our weakness. Amen.

Benediction

And now may the one who created you, redeemed you, and strengthens you be gracious to you in the midst of your weakness. Amen.

July 15, 2018

Passages: *2 Samuel 6:1-5,12b-19; Psalm 85:8-13; Ephesians 1:3-14; Mark 6:14-29*

Gathering Prayer

O God, we gather together today as your people, made holy through the grace and power revealed to us in Christ. Draw us together as your community, that we might discover our truest and fullest purpose in you. Amen.

Preaching Theme

Most preachers have a unique set of idiosyncratic tendencies when it comes to their preaching and their writing. Some use the same patterns of hand gestures and body movements to articulate their points. Some have favorite words or phrases that they use more than any other. Most preachers, after a while, ease into a writing and speaking style that becomes less about who they want to imitate and more a conscious expression of their authentic selves.

If one were to apply the same scrutiny to the Apostle Paul, there would be no mistaking what his favorite go-to phrase would be. It is the phrase "in Christ," found four times in this passage to the Ephesians alone (eight if one also counts "in him"), and ten times total, second only to 1 and 2 Corinthians. He uses it over seventy-five times in all of his writings, making it a chief element in his collection of favorite phrases.

Why is this phrase so meaningful to Paul? Marcus Borg and John Dominic Crossan suggest that the phrase explains Paul's abiding belief that Christianity is primarily a communal faith: "For Paul, life 'in Christ' was always a communal matter. This was so not simply because 'it's important to be part of a church,' but because his purpose, his passion, was to create communities whose life together embodied an alternative to the normalcy of the 'wisdom of this world.'"[1]

Paul used the words *in Christ* to describe more than a private, individual experience of Christ, but a communal, corporate experience within the body of believers. Whereas many religious mystical traditions require complete isolation, practicing transcendence in hermit-like seclusion, Paul believed that a mystical relationship with Christ was best experienced with fellow Christians, in a mutually caring, refining, and serving community.

To be "in Christ" is to be like a fish becoming aware of the water that is the very source of its life. It is an awareness that Paul best described to the people at the

Areopagus in Acts 17:28, where God is the one in whom we "live, move, and exist." For Paul, living "in Christ" meant nothing less than surrender and submission to the person and work of Jesus Christ, fully participating in his life, death, and resurrection.

The preacher might use this text from Ephesians by simply using all eight instances of "in Christ" and "in him" as the backbone of the sermon. What does each phrase suggest we have been given by God through Jesus Christ? How are those gifts best experienced in the context of Christian community, rather than in a private, individual experience? And how can one live in gratitude for those gifts?

Secondary Preaching Themes

The text from 2 Samuel is the story of the procession of the ark of the Lord and the corresponding jubilance that David demonstrated as he accompanied it. At first reading, this is a story that might seem odd, even archaic, to our modern ears. When is the last time any one of us can remember such a charismatic display of dancing, singing, and frivolity during a public religious ceremony?

Perhaps the nearest secular equivalent might be the procession of the Olympic torch to start an Olympic games. The torch originates in Athens, reminding everyone of the ancient roots of the games, in a kind of sacred/mythological nod to the gods of Greece. From there it crisscrosses the globe, passing through nearly every continent, carried by people who are privileged enough to touch it.

Then, during the final stretch, the torch enters the stadium, with shouts, acclamation, and festivity. And at the moment the official torch is lit to signal the start of the competitions, the stadium elevates to an uproar.

The preacher might simply ask the questions, "Why was David so filled with such feverish joy at the sight of the ark?" And what is preventing worshippers from assembling with that same kind of expectation and enthusiasm? When the acolyte brings in the light of Christ, or the crucifer enters bearing the cross of Christ, why aren't we filled with that same sense of awe, wonder, and excitement?

Prayer of Application

Gracious God, you have come into the world to be our salvation and to draw us into yourself. We remember that in you, we live, move, breathe, and have our being, and we become a community of mutual love and concern. Help us to be the people you have called us to be, that we might be filled with awe and excitement when we come to praise your name. Amen.

Benediction

Let us leave this place as one people, common in purpose, identity, and mission. May we be strengthened by the Spirit, as we remember that we are one in Christ. Amen.

July 22, 2018

Passages: *2 Samuel 7:1-14a; Psalm 23; Ephesians 2:11-22; Mark 6:30-34, 53-56*

Gathering Prayer

Gracious and loving God, we come to you as the crowds in the Gospels: hungry for hope, longing for love, yearning for a fresh experience of your power and love. As you meet us in this place, let us open our hearts to yours, that we might sense your compassion for us. Amen.

Preaching Theme

On rare occasions, the Gospel writers move from being objective sideline reporters to becoming intuitive mind readers, weaving together the actions of Jesus with his attitudes, and giving us a glimpse into his innermost motivations. One such passage is Mark's version of the feeding miracle.

Despite the fact that Jesus was trying to get away for a time of seclusion and rest, crowds of people were so determined to meet Jesus that they were already waiting at the deserted place when he arrived. And when Jesus saw them, Mark says that he had "compassion on them, because they were like sheep without a shepherd" (6:34).

The Greek word for "compassion" in this case literally means "gut-wrenching." Specifically, it is the word *splanchnidzomai*, and is related to the splanchnic nerve that connects to the stomach. For Jesus, seeing the needs of the crowd was a punch to his gut. His reaction was no mere pity; nor was it simply "feeling sorry for them." It was visceral and real, twisting his stomach in knots.

It might be easier to envision a Jesus who keeps his emotions in check, calmly and steadily aiding the masses with commendable efficiency. But Matthew and Mark are the only Gospels to share with us Jesus's gut-wrenching motive, in order to illustrate a point. Not only did Jesus minister to people but he also identified with their suffering. They were not simply anonymous victims, numbers on a roster, or appointments on a calendar. They were real people, with real stories, and real pain.

It is interesting that the lectionary at this point skips over the feeding miracle and moves to verses 53-56. Here, when Jesus arrives at Gennesaret, Jesus continues his healing ministry as more and more people are drawn to him. In fact, there are so many people who need his help, in so many different places, that Mark has to summarize the impact of Jesus by saying, "Wherever he went—villages, cities, or farming communities—they would place the sick in the marketplaces and beg him to allow them to touch even the hem of his clothing" (v. 56).

This is a stirring reminder of what ought to constitute the motivation of the church. What ought to drive the church forward in ministry is not a self-aggrandizing desire to grow bigger, or to gain more members, or to fund a larger budget, or to build grander buildings. Mark gives us a glimpse into the emotional state of Jesus for a reason: we need to have the compassion of Jesus if we are to carry on the work of Jesus.

We need to care for the needs of people in the community with the same kind of empathetic, gut-wrenching, loving compassion that moved Jesus. When that happens, the crowds will take notice. They will discover hope and security and the promise of new life in the good news of Jesus.

Secondary Preaching Themes

Perhaps there is no greater passage that can echo the themes found in the Gospel reading than the Twenty-Third Psalm. In this often quoted and memorized passage, the psalmist celebrates the way the Lord functions as his shepherd. This resonates with Jesus's compassion for the people who appear to him as "sheep without a shepherd."

The worship leader might choose to use this passage as a call to worship, or a liturgist may choose to use this as the basis for a congregational prayer. Each line offers a tender, pastoral reminder of the care that God gives to us, even in the valley of death's shadow. It concludes with a stirring vision of eternal glory, with goodness and mercy following us throughout our lives, with our permanent residence in the house of God.

Prayers from Biblical Women

God, you are our holy comforter, who cares for us as lost sheep without a shepherd. You fill us with your goodness, and mercy flows freely from your hand.

We confess to you our propensity to wander off on our own, seeking to take our lives into our own hands and provide for ourselves. We are a stubborn people, and we are prone to sin. Forgive us, Lord, and remind us of your compassion for us.

As we sense the love of your heart for us, empower us to be agents of compassion for others. Help us to seek those who are hurting, the lost sheep within our reach, and use us to gather them at your table. Amen.

Benediction

May the God of compassion reveal to you the way of love, that you may go from this place to reach out in concern and service to the world. As God calls you into new purpose, may you fulfill your calling in the world. Amen.

July 29, 2018

Passages: 2 Samuel 11:1-15; Psalm 145:10-18; Ephesians 3:14-21; John 6:1-21

Gathering Prayer

We come, hungry.

O Lord, fill our hearts with your love.

We come, prone to sin and temptation.

O Lord, assure us of our forgiveness and mercy.

We come, longing for purpose.

O Lord, use us to bless a hurting world.

Amen.

Preaching Theme

While the story of David and Bathsheba is widely known, it would be helpful to first remember how the story is set up in the previous chapter. In 2 Samuel 10, an enemy called the Ammoneans had risen up as a threat to Israel, and David mounted an offensive against them. In just a few days' fighting, David and the Israelite armies under his command were able to absolutely decimate the foreign forces.

To put it bluntly, David was on top of his game. He had crushed foreign armies, he had amassed great power and popularity, and he had it all. And all of this set David up to believe that he was in control of his own kingdom and master of his own life. He came to believe that he could have it all simply by exercising his own will, and he did not need to check his impulses against anything else or anyone else.

By the time we get to the whole lurid affair in chapter 11, we are set up to believe that the core issue for David was not lust. It was control. It was a deeply set belief that he could do anything he wanted, without regard to consequences, depending only on his strength.

In fact, take a look at the way that the writer of 2 Samuel puts it. Do you want to know how many times the name David occurs in the story of Bathsheba? Twenty-three times. And how many times is God's name mentioned? Zero.

This passage is not just about sexual immorality, although that might be the issue that many in the congregation may be facing. At its core, this story poses a question about what is at the center of one's life, and what is in one's heart. It would be good to remember the principle that introduces us to David in the first place: humans look at the outside, and God looks at the heart.

The question that the preacher may choose to pose for the congregation is whether or not we are willing to let God be in control of our passions, talents, and destiny, or whether we have fallen for the debilitating lie that all we have and all we can achieve is from your own initiative and strength. Because once we believe that, there is no stopping what harm we can do.

Once he learned that Bathsheba was pregnant, David sent for her soldier husband, Uriah, to come home from battle at once. He hoped that having them stay the night together might cover up the fact that Uriah was not the father. But when Uriah refused, David had him sent to the front lines of battle in order to be killed. And when Bathsheba became a widow, David married her.

Those who believe that they are in control of their lives often use that same power to cover up their sins, often making things worse. But God always has a way of seeing the things that we try to cover up.

Secondary Preaching Themes

In contrast to the selfishness of David, John shares a story of sacrificial self-giving as a model for our own generosity. When the hunger of the crowds had grown to a critical level, Jesus asked Philip for an assessment: "Where will we buy food to feed these people?" (John 6:5).

Philip's answer was realistic, though ultimately unhelpful. It was Andrew who stepped forward with a kind of creative solution that seemed at first to be woefully insignificant. A youth with five loaves and two fish.

This well-known story reminds us that even in the face of insurmountable challenges, God only requires of us faithfulness, obedience, and a willingness to take a risk. Unlike David, who saw only himself as the cause for overwhelming victories, the young boy saw self-giving generosity in the face of overwhelming odds.

Prayer of Confession

Loving God, we confess to you that we are all too human. We credit ourselves for the blessings that you give us. We convince ourselves that we are self-made creatures. We forget how we are utterly dependent on you. As a result, we are prone to temptation, and succumb too easily to sin.

Forgive us, Lord. In your infinite compassion and love, remind us of the better way, the purer way, that is found in your Son, Jesus. Just as the youth surrendered his means to the Messiah, we offer the fullness of our lives to you.

Take us, bless us, break us, and give us out in communion to the world. Amen.

Benediction

Go from this place in the power and love of God, so that you might be the means through which God blesses a starving world. Offer yourselves in selflessness and generosity, that God may be glorified through Jesus Christ, in whose name we pray, Amen.

August 5, 2018

Passages: 2 Samuel 11:26–12:13a; Psalm 78:23-29; Ephesians 4:1-6; John 6:24-35

Preaching Theme

King David remains in Jerusalem while his military elites capture cities in the region. He has become too important to be among the military while battles ensue. He stays in the palace and becomes very bored. One evening he stood on his balcony and while viewing the village below, he saw a beautiful woman bathing. David inquires as to her identity and realizes that she is the wife of Uriah, one of his military men, fighting a battle for him, while the king was lusting for his wife. David sends for her, takes her, lays with her, and returns her. Her name was Bathsheba.

What was intended to be a one-night stand, according to King David's manipulation and motivation, became the shame of covering up Bathsheba's pregnancy. Bathsheba notifies David that she is with child, and David's plotting turns into violence and death.

King David makes the death of Uriah possible and makes sure that Bathsheba receives a report of her husband's death. Bathsheba mourns and grieves Uriah's death after proper burial. Then David brings Bathsheba to the palace and eventually marries her, and they have a son.

The prophet Nathan delivers a message to David from God. God's message was that God had saved David from Saul and given him the wives and palace of Saul and both the kingdoms of Judah and Israel. God was disappointed that David would disrespect the laws of God after all that he had accomplished. God punished David by allowing him to live, but his family would rebel against him, and his wives would be given to other men who will take them to bed publicly.

We are reminded that what is done in secret will be done in the open and in the sight of all Israel. God gives attention to our behavior because God's reputation is reflected in our conduct. David did not repent until God sent Nathan to confront him about his sin. Then David admitted to his sin and repented. David did not initiate restoration of fellowship with God and did not acknowledge the sin of rebellion against God's commandments that adultery and murder are wrong. We cannot make excuses or ignore our wrongful ways but must confess to God that we have sinned against God and ask for forgiveness to receive God's grace.

While God forgives and allows us to repent and restore our relationship back to God, David's ultimate punishment was the death of David and Bathsheba's first son, for he broke the laws of God. Obedience is an important part of our relationship with God.

Secondary Preaching Themes

Ephesians 4:1-6

We are reminded in Ephesians 4 that our actions are to be godly and that we are to "walk worthy of the calling" (v. 1, NKJV). To walk worthy defines the type of life we are to live so as to please and honor God for we are chosen to do good works. God has a calling to find and call others who will be devoted to the laws of God. That is God's calling, and our calling is to uphold God's laws. God desires our faithfulness and obedience.

The virtues are essential for us to use to be successful in building and maintaining the body of Christ. The virtues of humbleness, gentleness, and patience distinctly define this community as Christians in "light" and not darkness. The virtues are a prelude to our instructions telling us to "[bear] with one another in love." For love is a major foundation that shows us how to relate to one another. Such love shifts us to place our attention on the "unity of the Spirit" and the "bond of peace," for love pulls everything together and creates harmony (vv. 2-3, NKJV).

Psalm 78:23-29

Again we are referred to God's character as a God of provisions and the God of the faithful followers. Psalm 78:23-29, in today's times, warns us against being unsatisfied when our God provides our every need.

John 6:24-35

God tells us that God is life and that we are to have faith and believe and not be dependent on earthly nourishment. All of our nourishment is to come to us from God through Jesus as the conduit. We are expected to have faith and recognize that God is God and that we are not God. As God provides for us, we are to show humility and not lack appreciation like the Israelites in the desert who challenged God regarding their needs and requests. While we do God's work, it is important to look at ourselves and note our brokenness and imperfection.

Prayer of Confession

God of Mercy,

We plead for your mercy.

We acknowledge and confess our sins.

A pure heart is what we desire and pray that you will deliver to us.

Have mercy on us according to your unconditional love

Wash away our sins, for you are compassionate and slow to anger.

With your everlasting love forgive our wickedness and our rebellious and sinful ways.

Discipline us as you restore our relationship.

Blot out our transgressions,

Wash away our iniquity,

Cleanse us from our sin

In Jesus's name,

Amen.

August 12, 2018

Passages: *2 Samuel 18:5-9, 15, 31-33; Psalm 34:1-8; Ephesians 4:25–5:2; John 6:35, 41-51*

Gathering Litany (based on Psalm 34)

We will bless the LORD at all times; his praise will always be in our mouths.

Praise the Lord—let the suffering listen and rejoice.

Magnify the LORD! Together let us lift his name up high!

We sought the Lord and he answered us. God delivered us from all our fears.

Those who look to God will shine;

Their faces are never ashamed.

Preaching Theme

The lectionary spends most of the month of August in John 6. Preachers who base their sermons on the Gospel text this month may soon find themselves running dry on imagery and stories related to bread! John 6 is a long chapter, but it has a singular theme related to what is true food and who brings—and literally embodies—the true bread that alone nourishes us for eternal life. In the lection for this Sunday, Jesus makes one of his famous "I Am" sayings and indicates that he himself has "come down from heaven."

This, in turn, elicits incredulity from those listening to him. It's another version of the locals sneering at the hometown boy for thinking more highly of himself than he ought. "Who does *he* think he is? 'Come down from heaven!' Right! We all know he came from just down the block and well recall when he was knee-high to a grasshopper. Give us a break on this 'heaven' business!"

For his part, Jesus is more open and blunt than usual. He tells these folks to hush up and stop their grumbling and sneering and then directly tells them that he alone represents their only shot at true life. He has seen the Father, comes from the Father, and now offers the true bread that only the Father above can give. Take it or leave it. The original wonder bread of manna came down from heaven by God's own hand, but the people who ate it still died by and by. But not with the stuff Jesus has to offer.

In fact, what Jesus has to offer is his very flesh (and stay tuned for next week's lectionary text to see the reaction to those startling and scandalous words).

C. S. Lewis once famously said that when it comes to Jesus you have a choice: chalk him up as a raving lunatic as nutty as someone who claims to be a poached egg or embrace him as the only true Savior who was sent here by God himself to save the world. There is really no middle ground here (and so away with those who reject Jesus's claims to divinity but still esteem him as a "good teacher" or a moral example or something). The choice is a stark one, and John 6 makes that clear. Preaching on this text should do no less.

Secondary Preaching Themes

When we read New Testament letters, we need to be reminded again and again that we are reading someone else's mail. We have only one-half of the correspondence in any event and so cannot always know what gave rise to this or that thing Paul or any other author jotted down. In the case of Ephesians 4–5, it becomes clear that Paul had to urge people to get rid of lingering anger, to stop stealing, to stop using foul language because, as a matter of fact, he had gotten wind that precisely this was happening in Ephesus.

But how can it be that members of the church were stealing things? Granted, none of us is perfect, but we don't usually assume that active robbers are in the congregation. But something was behind Paul's words here and the simplest explanation is that in various forms, professing Christians were stealing things. It's a sobering reminder of how the battle with our sinfulness is ongoing. If we are honest, we know that anger is an issue. Parachute into any given congregation and it won't take long to find out which members refuse to sit near or speak to other members of the church. And there are lots of ways to snooker and steal from one another.

But this just cannot be, Paul urges. Baptism was supposed to drown all that out. Following Christ is supposed to mean living sacrificially as Christ did. We fool ourselves if we think we are not engaged in a lifelong battle with sin. If we take to ourselves the true bread of life in the Lord's Supper, then that is supposed to nourish us so we can grow up big and strong and Christlike. We need to be reminded of this again and again, no matter how uncomfortable the naming of such topics may make us.

Benediction (from Ephesians 5)

May the spirit of God enable you to live as Christ lived, following the example of Jesus who gave himself for us as a sweet offering to God, and may that sweet aroma permeate your lives, your homes, and the entire world.

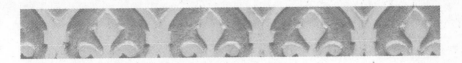

August 19, 2018

Passages: 1 Kings 2:10-20; 3:3-14; Psalm 34:9-14; Ephesians 5:12-20; John 6:51-58

Opening Prayer (from Ephesians 5)

Dear God, in this time of worship and at all times, move us to speak to each other in psalms, hymns, and spiritual songs. Fill us with the sweet wine of your Spirit so that the melody of our lives will be pleasing to you and edifying for one another. And in everything may we make thanksgiving to you in gratitude for all that you give us through Christ Jesus our Lord and Savior. Amen.

Preaching Theme

In her short story "The River," Flannery O'Connor depicts a child who drowns when trying to baptize himself in a river. After this startling story was published, someone asked O'Connor about this grotesque depiction of baptism. O'Connor's critics thought this story was too extreme. But her goal was to remind her readers of how vividly powerful baptism is, that the Bible really does tell us it involves the death of the old self and the resurrection of a new self in Christ. So when people criticized her for such a startling depiction, O'Connor said in essence that in the land of the nearly blind, you need to draw really big caricatures.

In John 6, Jesus seems determined to magnify the shock value of his words via the specific vocabulary he used. Up until verse 54 he had used the more ordinary Greek word for "to eat" (*phagein*), but in verse 54—seemingly in reaction to the questions being raised by the crowd—he toggles over to the lesser-used verb of *trogein*, which appears to have carried with it the connotation of "chewing with your mouth open." Picture a cow chewing his cud. Picture an elementary school child smacking up a peanut butter and jelly sandwich, her mouth yawning open widely between each smacking chew.

This is intentional on John's part, magnifying the vividness of the real "feeding" that takes place in the Eucharistic meal. If you chew with your mouth open, there is no doubting the food that is in your mouth. You cannot pretend to be chewing something if people can see into your mouth. That kind of eating shows you the real deal, the actual substance of what's in a person's mouth.

So in one sense Jesus may have been purposely exaggerating the "Yuck!" factor here. He has already knocked people off kilter by suggesting something that sounds vaguely cannibalistic and now seems intent on making that already gross-sounding scenario more intensely repugnant. Jesus is not bandying around empty words or rhetoric.

No, what Jesus is talking about really is a matter of life or death. To have any life worth talking about, you really do need to enter into the life of the Father through the Son. What Jesus is offering here is nothing short of an access to the life of the tri-une God. Think of that! Jesus is saying that union with him (signified by Eucharistic participation in Christ) allows us to enter into the rhythms of Father, Son, and Holy Spirit, into the life that existed before anything like the creation existed and that even now is the bright center to everything in the universe.

Secondary Preaching Themes

In the landmark film *The Godfather*, the mafia kingpin Don Vito Corleone at one point makes peace with the heads of the five major crime families in New York. In order to secure the safety of his younger son, the Don swears he will forego the vengeance he could exact for the murder of his oldest son. The Don swears that in his lifetime, no acts of revenge would come. The peace is made and it holds until...the Don dies. Before he dies he instructs his younger son on the need to settle the old scores after all. And not long after the old man's death, that is exactly what the son does, killing all five heads of the other families.

Well, that's a violent mafia movie and you'd think it has little to do with the Bible until you get to 1 Kings 2 and the first nine verses that the lectionary would actually have you skip over. But there the dying King David gives gruesome instructions to his heir apparent son Solomon on who to rub out after his death on account of the crimes and treasons they had committed. David won't touch them, but Solomon...well, it's a time to settle old scores apparently. This is one of those Bible passages that is rated R.

It may be a little tough to spy the gospel in a text as saturated with bad news and violence as the early chapters of 1 Kings are, but it's surely not too tough to spy the *need* for a gospel of good news and grace in these chapters. Given the prominence of wisdom in these same chapters, it's also not too tough to spot that Wisdom incarnate is going to be exactly what this tired and violent old world will need in the end.

August 26, 2018

Passages: 1 Kings 8: (1, 6, 10-11) 22-30, 41-43; Psalm 34:15-22;
Ephesians 6:10-20; John 6:56-69

Opening Litany (based on Psalm 34)

The Lord's eyes watch the righteous, he listens to their cries.

When the righteous cry out, God listens and delivers them from their troubles.

The Lord is close to the brokenhearted, he saves those whose spirits are crushed.

Our lives are full of troubles, but the Lord sees us and delivers us.

The Lord loves all those who take refuge in him.

The Lord is our strength, our refuge, our deliverer. Praise the Lord!

Preaching Theme

For Jesus to say, "I am the bread of life," wasn't too scandalous. Jesus was known as a great teacher and so here appears to be comparing his words to bread, to a kind of spiritual cuisine that could feed your soul. Had Jesus stopped there, things may have gone better. But next thing you know, Jesus says that the bread in question is not his teaching but his own flesh. Getting a bit more graphic yet, Jesus says that what you needed to wash down his flesh was a cup brimming with some of his blood.

This is where Jesus lost a lot of the crowd. Jesus lost them because he was making them lose their lunch. It was disgusting! Of course, as he makes clear after most of the crowd had fled, he really was being metaphorical. But if the metaphor was strong, it was only because the reality behind the metaphor was stronger still. But the only way you are going to accept such a startling teaching is if Jesus's Father reveals it to you. But lots of people did not want to stick with a man who talked that way, and so they left.

Then, in a touching verse, Jesus turns to his disciples with moist eyes and with a quivering chin. "Do you also want to leave?" he asks quietly. Peter's answer is even more moving than the question. "Lord, where would we go? **You** have the words of eternal life." It's the gift of faith that shows you that. "No one comes to the Father except through me," Jesus says.

Today as long ago, Jesus still asks, "Do you also want to leave??" As preachers, we want to help make it the case that the members of our congregations will always be able to say in reply to this question, "And just where would we go, Lord? You have the words of life!"

Secondary Preaching Themes

A major theme in John's Gospel is Jesus as the true temple. He himself is that dwelling of God with humanity that the old temple represented and, in John 6, Jesus also makes clear that the same body that is the true temple is also the true bread and drink that nourishes for eternal life. So it is fitting that the lectionary pairs this final text from John 6 with 1 Kings 8 and Solomon's dedication of the original temple in Jerusalem. It is fitting because as with Jesus, so Solomon makes clear that the truest purpose of the temple is not exclusion but inclusion, a desire to draw all people to God.

Solomon makes sure to include all people in his prayer and so sent a signal to all who heard him that day that although Israel may have been the singular dwelling place for the Most High God at that time, Israel could never quite claim ownership of that God any more than they had private access to him. Ultimately this universalizing of the people of God comes to its fullest expression in Christ and through his gospel.

"Will God really dwell on the earth?" Solomon asked long ago. The gospel gives us the ultimate answer to that question by showing Jesus of Nazareth dwelling among us, full of grace and truth. But if Solomon was right that the open eyes of God would always be upon his temple in Jerusalem, then we can know for sure that those same open eyes are upon the people of God today too—on **all** God's people in all places. As the old hymn puts it, in Christ there is no east or west, no north or south. No one is denied access to the one true God in Christ. No matter who you are, no matter where you are, no matter where you came from, when you pray to God, that God listens. He listens, for his name alone really is great.

Benediction

May your open eyes, O God, be always on us your people. May we live in such a way to make clear that the true bread of life that is the body of our Lord is given so that all may find eternal life. Bless us, dear Father, that we might be a blessing and send us out with your peace in the name of the Father, and of the Son, and of the Holy Spirit, Amen.

September 2, 2018

Passages: Song of Solomon 2:8-13; Psalm 15; James 1:17-27; Mark 7:1-8, 14-15, 21-23

Gathering Prayer

Behold your church, Lord Jesus! We gather before you in this place carrying our hopes and holding our ambitions. Free us from worries. Release us from our fears. With hope in our hearts and a longing for your Spirit we come seeking to be remade in and through your love so that we might be faithful disciples. In your name we pray, Amen.

Preaching Theme

Let love go! Don't let anything stop you from releasing God's goodness in your life and into the world around you. Don't let social conventions, customs, or habits get in the way of following Jesus by loving the people around you. You don't need any special talents or big projects to fill the world with the love of Jesus. Our faith is expressed in how we conduct our business and make our living. Love is released when we speak up for the vulnerable, keep our promises to our friends, and refuse to profit at someone else's expense. James (likely the brother of Jesus) gives examples of how God's people are to let love go: let's listen more than we talk! "Lead with your ears, follow up with your tongue," says Eugene Peterson in *The Message* (James 1:19).[1] Don't allow little things to get under your skin. Talk is cheap. And religious talk might be the cheapest stuff out there. It's all about backing it up with your life. This is love taking shape in the world through our words and deeds. We don't will ourselves into becoming good. We become good by studying the one who is good. James learned the way of Jesus by living with his brother, working alongside him, watching his day-to-day interactions. We still learn in the same way. We learn by watching the way of Jesus and then allowing that goodness to permeate us, thereby making us good. While visiting the city of Avila years ago, I picked up a prayer card with a line attributed to the mystic writer St. Teresa of Avila that said "Let Love love you." We become doers of the living word of Christ when we welcome love into all arenas of life. It's the power of love that "has the power to save" our souls, as James writes in verse 21 (NRSV).

Secondary Preaching Themes

Ah, amore! The sweet freshness and sudden passion of young love echo God's desire for us. We may try to spiritualize the text in this Song of Solomon by naming Jesus as the lily of the valley (2:1) and the lover upon whom we await (2:4-8). But the sheer physicality and incarnation of love keeps seeping through. This is the dawn of desire for another. With the freshness of spring as the backdrop, a young couple is beaconed to join the song of nature in lovemaking and joy. It is a celebration of love all around us.

"Do what I say, not what I do" is a wail we have heard not just from our parents but from our own lips. We have all felt the rub of saying one thing and doing something entirely different. Paul's words from Romans 7:14-20 reverberate in us daily. Congruence can be difficult to see. Researchers say one way to build congruence is to regularly list the six most obvious gaps between what we say and what we do. Then ask a colleague or friend to list what they see as the six most obvious gaps. And reflect on the two lists side by side. James urges us to go one step further by comparing this newfound knowledge to the example of Jesus.

It's easy to overthink discipleship. We struggle to find the exact parallels to the Jewish dietary and sanitation laws. Just how do we apply laws about cleaning drinking glasses and washing our hands to our twenty-first-century lives? Our struggle has caused us to forbid such things as playing cards or dining out on Sunday. We seek the clear bright lines the law offered us since we want to know what is in or outside the line. But discipleship is richer. Discipleship is both simple and difficult at the same time. Mother Teresa had two "simple" rules for following Jesus. She first made the decision that she would refuse God nothing. Whatever God asked of her she would do. The second rule is that when the Lord asked her she would obey God without delay. No overthinking. No getting it all nailed down. Mother Teresa just started moving as soon as the Lord called. Clarification would happen while she was on the way.

Confession (based on *A Prayer for Guidance* by Thomas Merton)

My Lord God, We have no idea where we are going.

We do not sense the road ahead of us.

Nor do we really know ourselves.

And the fact that we think we are following your will does not mean we are actually doing so.

But we do believe that the desire to please you,

Does in fact please you.

Therefore we will trust you always, though we may seem to be lost and in the shadow of death.

We will not fear, for you are ever with us. And you will never leave us to face our struggles alone.

September 9, 2018

Passages: Proverbs 22:1-2, 8-9, 22-23; Psalm 146; James 2:1-10 (11-13); Mark 7:24-37

Call to Worship

People of the Living God, come and praise the Lord!

We will sing to the Lord as long as we live!

Sing praises to God your whole life long.

Happy are those whose hope is in the Lord our God; who made heaven and earth, the sea and all that is in them.

For God has set the prisoners free and opened the eyes of the blind.

The Lord has lifted the downcast and loves the righteous;

God watches over the strangers;

and protects the orphan and widow.

The Lord will reign forever.

Praise the Lord!

Praise the Lord. Praise the Lord forever!

Preaching Theme

Popular magazines as distinct as *People* to *Vogue* bear witness to a commonly accepted truth: the rich have it all. The only thing better than being rich is being young, beautiful, and rich. James understood how attractive these people seem to us regular folks. He knew that the wealthy seem to have the life we want. We give the rich special seats and special attention to court their favor.

It's no use denying it. Even if we personally believe that we are impervious to the temptation of wealth, our society gives us away. As twenty-first-century Americans, we rank among the most powerful and the most prosperous people ever to walk the earth. For those who don't believe in their wealth, a quick visit to globalrichlist.com can reveal how your income compares with the income of others throughout the world.

Yet even for us in America, we can feel the ground underneath us giving way. This is our reality: In January 2016, Oxfam reported that sixty-three of the world's richest billionaires control as much wealth as 50 percent of the world's poorest population. The 2015 Global Wealth Databook reveals 1 percent of the world's population own more wealth than 99 percent of the world's people. None of us would likely say we are actively "dishonoring" the poor (v. 6), yet at some point we must ask the question whether our system itself dishonors them.

In the midst of many fawning on the rich, Jesus had a special place for the poor. He traveled through Tyre and Sidon, places where non-Jews lived; towns of the nameless and the powerless. There he was willing to be challenged by a destitute foreigner and heal a deaf Gentile. Their faith in the Savior stood as a witness to the faithlessness of Israel. While our society testifies to the power of wealth and celebrity, the poor bear witness to the truth that *you never know God is all you need until God is all you have.*

Today the towns of Tyre and Sidon are part of Lebanon, a country that has been straining to host the two million Syrian refugees who have poured into their borders desperate to escape the violence in their own country. These refugees are nameless to most of us. Yet throughout the settlements one finds the church of Christ—teaching in popup schools, dispensing medicines in the clinics, and distributing food and water. They are followers of Christ who are providing a "special place" not to the rich but the poor, living in the way James outlines.

Secondary Preaching Themes

Proverbs 22:8-9

The Proverbs texts direct us to trust in God even when we would rather trust in our own resources. The wisdom of Proverbs 22:8-9 discusses our tendency to hold tightly on to things we believe are ours. We may believe our "rod of . . . fury" was justly acquired, yet when we hold on to that anger, we become unjust. We may believe our money and resources are all ours to do with what we please. But the writer reminds us that we receive blessings *after* we have shared.

Psalm 146

Psalm 146 echoes this trustful dependency in the Eternal One. Don't trust that others are going to do the right thing, make the right decision, or even fulfill the duties of their jobs. Heads of state ("princes" in verse 3 [NRSV]) may not act rightly, and at some point friends and family are going to be either unwilling or unable to help. The only trustworthy one is God, who is constant and unchanging.

Mark 7:24-37

Jesus initially denies the woman's request because he has come to heal Israel first. Her counter assertion to Jesus "even the dogs under the table eat the children's crumbs" employs a turn of phrase used by a Greco-Roman philosophical movement called the Cynics (often called "dogs"). The Cynics were famous for using their wit to undermine social norms.

A popular social media meme shows the vastly different ways bypassers respond to a young girl on the streets of New York City. When the ten-year-old is dressed as a homeless girl, she is actively shooed away from lunch tables and ignored as she stands crying on the sidewalk. But when her clothes are changed to designer wear, concerned strangers offer all they can—even calling the police and waiting with her until they arrive.

Benediction

Children of the living God, what does the Lord require of you but to do justice, love mercy, and to walk humbly with your God. Go and walk in the way of Jesus, trusting that his work in you is sufficient. Amen.

September 16, 2018

Passages: Proverbs 1:20-33; Psalm 116:1-9; James 3:1-12; Mark 8:27-38

Gathering Prayer (based on a Ghanaian hymn)

Wake up soul; come and praise your God.

Wake up spirit for your God deserves thanks.

All the animals wake up to praise God.

All those who fly wake up to praise God.

Human soul, spring up and praise your God.

Let everything that breathes, praise the Lord!

Preaching Theme

What we say matters. Words, whether thoughtfully or carelessly spoken, tell something about our hopes and expectations, or our convictions and fears. Perhaps no disciple understood the power of the tongue more than Peter. With his words he pledged passionate allegiance to Jesus only to soon utter words of fear and betrayal. With his tongue he boldly declared his growing awareness that Jesus was the Son of God and Son of Man, and with his words he revealed his lack of understanding and fear about the mission of Jesus. Our words can reveal truths and emotions we didn't even know we had. How many of us have answered a casual question with a burst of energy and passion we didn't know was in us? *What was that all about?* we wonder. Or who hasn't had the experience of belting out an angry sarcasm in what was (until then) a pretty ordinary conversation? Perhaps Peter didn't know the depth of his unease and the limitations of his convictions until he uttered them out loud. "You are the Messiah!" he blurts out. Ah! There it is—*This is what I've been sensing!* These words of Peter give Jesus something to work with. The expression of Peter's heart is now *out there.* And this previously nascent sense can now be honed, focused, and challenged by questions and conversations with Jesus.

Peter's internal understanding can now be corrected too. This is the way it is with us, isn't it? Jesus desires that we engage with him—not only internally in our hearts but with what we put out there in the world. Jesus wasn't only interested in what others said about him; he wanted to know what his disciples said of him too. Regularly, repeatedly, Jesus asked his disciples to engage with him by voicing what they were feeling and thinking. Our fumbling for the words and searching for the phrase is all fodder for Jesus to use as he clarifies, polishes, and crafts us as disciples. Words. They matter.

Secondary Preaching Themes

The streets of downtown Chicago are filled with people shouting to get your attention. "Store closing! Everything must go!" "Please, give to the homeless!" Speakers and messages vying for our time and our limited resources. Proverbs opens with wisdom crying out to us in a similar manner. Using a megaphone to amplify her voice above the fray: Give heed! Listen to me! Wisdom at times speaks like an angry prophet urging a return to holiness (chapter 1) or a hostess inviting guests to eat at her banquet table (chapter 9), but always she tries to entice people consumed with worries and cares to stop and listen to the divine words that lead to life.

Speaking as a spiritual practice has long been a way by which disciples become mature followers of Christ. By intentionally not speaking during some hours of the day, Christians become more aware of their words when they do speak. In a world eager for buzz, formed by flippant comments and reactive remarks, carefully choosing our words is downright counter-cultural.

In the film *Into Great Silence*, Philip Groning explores life inside a Carthusian monastery in the French Alps. Six days a week the monks are silent, speaking only occasionally on their Monday walks. The rest of the week their only words are said during the songs and prayers of their worship. This has been the pattern of the Carthusians since 1084. The film is rooted in the slow, unfolding rhythms of day and night: working and praying, eating and sleeping, the slow aging of the monks' bodies and the gentle rise and fall of the seasons. *Into Great Silence* gives us an opportunity to contemplate the holy rhythms of our lives, allowing us to see patterns and cadences we may be too busy to notice.

Confession (based on Psalm 19)

May the words of our mouths and the meditation of our hearts be pleasing to you our God.

For you are our rock and redeemer. You are the source of our strength.

Your words pull our life together and make us whole.

Your words our God speak of life.

Your words speak of the life we desire.

We desire a life of truth and generosity; a life holy and just.

May our words mirror your words our God.

May we too speak words of truth and generosity.

Words of life! Holy and just.

May the words of my mouth and the meditation of my heart be pleasing to you my God.

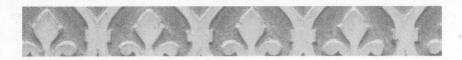

September 23, 2018

Passages: Proverbs 31:10-31; Psalm 54; James 3:13–4:3; Mark 9:30-37

Call to Worship

Rejoice in the Lord always; again I will say, rejoice!

Let your gentleness be known to everyone.

The Lord is near.

Preaching Theme

Mine! No, mine! Give it to me now! Words familiar to any parent. Children have a knack for perceiving when someone else is getting more ice cream or more attention. They have a built-in sonar for the exact number of M&M's given or how many books were read. They know who last got a "special treat" or sat in the front seat. Children keep score. So it is surprising and ironic that in a power struggle when the disciples are behaving like children, Jesus unmasks their aspiration to power by putting a real child in their midst and using him as an object lesson. And what an object lesson it is! *"Whoever welcomes a child in my name, welcomes me."* Coming as it does on the heels of Jesus's healing a Syrophonecian woman's daughter and a deaf and mute son, many see this sequence as Jesus radically aligning his kingdom with the least and the last rather than the most and the first. Jesus turns over the social order. Leadership and power will rise from the bottom up.

"Leading from Behind," a leadership model championed by Harvard Business School professor Linda Hill, echoes some of Jesus's thoughts. Leadership is viewed as a collaborative activity. Nelson Mandela in *Long March to Freedom* articulated his leadership in this model: "A leader . . . is like a shepherd. He stays behind the flock, letting the most nimble go out ahead, whereupon the others follow, not realizing that all along they are being directed from behind."[2] Leadership is viewed as a collaborative activity, not as a means to make your name great. The dynamic of power continues into the next section, verses 38-39 (outside the lectionary scope), where John wishes to maintain a monopoly over who can exercise power "in Jesus's name." John's criticism of the successful exorcist (a feat the disciples were incapable of doing in Mark 9:14-29) was based on the fact that the man "wasn't following *us.*" The disciples wanted someone following them more than they wanted to follow. How many of us desire the same thing?

Secondary Preaching Themes

1 Samuel 23:1-20

What do we do when we're attacked? More specifically, what do we do when those we had helped and befriended attack us? Betrayal is what David is experiencing in this psalm. The evil men and strangers (v. 3) are the very ones David had saved from the Philistines (1 Sam 23:1-20). The expected thing would be to strike back. Instead David remembers that this is not the first time he has been vulnerable. And in assurance of God's help David goes ahead to give a freewill offering of thanksgiving. No self-defense necessary. God's got this.

James 3:13–4:3

James advises us to run our desires through the filter of wisdom. Actions done in a humility that is borne of wisdom show us the good life God desires. How interesting that humility and wisdom are so directly paired. Is it because the more we examine our own lives, the more humble we become? Perhaps. Repeated practiced attention to our lives is what James advocates. He urges us to examine the deeper source of our disagreements (it's rarely what's on the surface!) and the underlying assumptions of our desires. Our conflicts, disagreements, and discord can be places of growth and wisdom.

St. Ignatius of Loyola is well known for his *Prayer of Examen*, a bedrock of Jesuit spirituality. The *Prayer of Examen* is based on five movements: First, intentionally place yourself in God's presence. Give thanks for God's great love for you. Secondly, pray for the grace to understand how God is working in your life. The next step is the heart of the prayer as you review your day—recalling specific moments and your feelings at the time. There is no moment too trivial or too painful that God was not involved with. Next, reflect on what you did, said, or thought in those instances. Ask yourself, were you drawing closer to God, or further away? Finally, with gratitude look toward tomorrow and consider how you might collaborate more effectively with God. Be specific. Conclude with the Lord's Prayer.

Prayer of Confession

Holy and generous God,

You are the giver of all good things.

All good things are sent from heaven above.

Rain and sun, day and night, justice and righteousness.

Bread to the eater and seed to the sower.

Peace to the old, energy to the young, joy to the babies.

But we are takers, who take from you, gracious God. Taking all we need as you supply.

And then taking more,

Taking more than we need. Taking what is not ours.

Taking the dignity of others.

Taking from the bounty of the earth.

Taking without thought. Taking without giving.

But you God are the giver of all good things.

We want to learn how to give like you.

Teach us how to give—not take.

So that we may give with joy and gladness.

So that others may receive.

So that others may know you are the giver of all good things.

September 30, 2018

Passages: *Esther 7:1-6, 9-10; 9:20-22; Psalm 19:7-14; James 5:13-20; Mark 9:38-50*

Gathering Prayer

O God of hope, we ask for eyes to see you today. In the soft hues of morning light, shine out the glory of your presence. In the living power of your word, speak anew in ways that reshape our longings and our lives. Over the clash of the world's empires, let us hear the echoes of your coming kingdom. We would be encountered by you today and so shaped that as we live this week, others would encounter you through us. Amen.

Preaching Theme

Esther is the story of God's silent sovereignty and as such is a parable of hope for all who struggle with the hiddenness of God in a world gone wrong. Entering at the climax of the plot, the lectionary's sole treatment of the book of Esther reminds us, in Karen Jobes's words, that God is omnipotently present where he is most conspicuously absent. There is deliverance even without a discernable deliverer. Yet the contours of that deliverance echo the deep contours of sin and salvation. Discovering that even the hidden God cannot be mocked, Haman who has treacherously sown the wind now reaps the whirlwind. And Esther, in her identification with the life and fate of her people, foreshadows God's ultimate solution to the evils of the world. Though often obscured by sin, God breaks into human history through the silent body (Isa 53:7) of a crucified Savior who became sin for us that we might experience the eternal deliverance of God. Esther thus reminds us that God is in control, bending the arc of history toward redemption for us and, in the mystery of grace, through us.

Secondary Preaching Themes

God is the great communicator as deft with speaking through the warmth of sunbeams and the songs of skylarks as with gerund phrases and adverbial clauses.

An ode to the cosmic communicator, Psalm 19 is in C. S. Lewis's estimation "the greatest Poem in the Psalter and one of the greatest lyrics in the world."[3] Verses 1-6 lyricize God's great revelation through creation while verses 7-10 celebrate God's perfect speech in scripture. Yet a celebration of God's speech is also a call for human listening, and so the psalm concludes with a prayer of confession, naming our perennial deafness to the pied beauty of God's living voice.

Confronting the dullness of human hearts, Christ in Mark 9 amps up the volume. A cascade of unsettling images (millstones, severed limbs, gouged-out eyes, devouring worms and fire) conspire to wake listeners from the stupor of sin into the dawning glory of God's kingdom. At the center of that kingdom is the name of Christ, through which believers will discern new partnerships in ministry and new value in small acts like cups of cold water given in the name of the one who gave himself.

In almost surprising fashion, the most practical book in the New Testament ends with a call to prayer and confession. Such ecclesiastical postures may seem out of place with James's progressive piety of caring for orphans and widows. Yet perhaps they are the best. For the power to make a difference in the world is not sourced in us. In confession we name our own need for the Savior we would be. In prayer we dialogue with the one who truly listens and heals.

Prayer of Confession

Gracious God, you invite us out of the hermitage of our shame into the honesty of grace. From hiding behind the masks of Sunday perfection, draw us into the freedom of being found and yet still loved. Grant us the boldness to confess our sins to one another and so from the isolation of hypocrisy bring us anew into the restorative community of those who know and together celebrate your grace. For we pray this in Jesus's name. Amen.

Responsive Reading (from Psalm 19)

Leader: Heaven is declaring God's glory; the sky is proclaiming his handiwork.

People: Of course, there's no speech, no words—their voices can't be heard—

Leader: but their sound extends throughout the world; their words reach the ends of the earth.

People: The Lord's instruction is perfect, reviving one's very being.

Leader: The LORD's laws are faithful, making naive people wise.

People: The Lord's regulations are right, gladdening the heart.

Leader: The LORD's commands are pure, giving light to the eyes.

People: They are more desirable than gold—than tons of pure gold!

Leader: No doubt about it: your servant is enlightened by them; there is great reward in keeping them.

People: Let the words of my mouth and the meditations of my heart be pleasing to you, Lord, my rock and my redeemer.

Benediction

May the peace of God

so settle on your soul,

that in the silence of faith

you may hear the creator

rejoicing over you with singing.

October 7, 2018

*Passages: Job 1:1; 2:1-10; Psalm 8; Hebrews 1:1-4; 2:5-12;
Mark 10:2-16*

Call to Worship (based on Hebrews 1)

Leader: In the past, God spoke through the prophets to our ancestors in many times and many ways.

People: In these final days, though, he spoke to us through a Son.

Leader: He is . . .

People: the heir of everything through whom the world was made.

Leader: He is . . .

People: the light of God's glory and the imprint of God's being.

Leader: He is . . .

People: the one who maintains everything with his powerful message.

Leader: He is . . .

People: our Savior who carried out the cleansing of people from their sins.

Leader: He is . . .

People: the one who sat down at the right side of the highest majesty. Hallelujah!

Preaching Theme

In soaring language, Hebrews begins with a sunburst of high Christology as the book's unknown author seeks to make Jesus known. The opening four-verse prologue is a polemic in poetry, introducing in seven ways the superiority of Christ that will be the key theme of a book in which the word *better* occurs a dozen times. In Hebrews there is no messianic secret. History is awash in the gracious speech of God. In the cool of the garden and over the chaos of the flood, through a burning bush and a pagan's donkey, by prophetic object lesson and oracle, God has spoken "in many times and in many ways." But it is in the last days that God speaks God's clearest word. Through the incarnate glory of divine radiance refracted off the bleeding brow of a Jewish carpenter, the imprint of God's very being is manifest and the purification of God's people from their sins is accomplished.

But the God who speaks is also to be heard. And so chapter 2 begins with the first of five warnings in the book not to "drift away." Gripped by the seduction of nostalgia, Hebrews's original audience perhaps found lofty Christology to be less compelling than manageable spirituality. More approachable angels, visible priests, and reoccurring sacrifices presented a compelling alternative to the humbling intangibles of grace. But it is grace, Hebrews reminds us, that we need. Quoting Psalm 8, the author further reminds us that God's crowning glory can come in undeservedly small packages. And in the surprise of the gospel, the superior glory of the Christ was won not with angelic harps, but with a hellish death. That is grace: "He's the one who is now crowned with glory and honor because of the suffering of his death. He suffered death so that he could taste death for everyone through God's grace" (Heb 2:9).

Secondary Preaching Themes

Job confronts us with theodicy as drama, and today's verses are the prologue to that painful play. The opening verses present a great earthly tragedy with a troubling cosmic backdrop. God and the adversary make a bet, and Job is the collateral damage. So begins a journey into humanity's deepest questions through one man's deepest griefs. Yet from the ashes of tragedy shines the rugged beauty of faith. Grasping more than his broken piece of pottery, Job holds on to a God whose rule he still accepts but no longer understands.

We live in a world bathed in glory. From steam rising off a newborn fawn in a spring meadow to the cold grandeur of the Orion Nebula, creation conspires to elicit both praise and awe from the created. Psalm 8 is praise that both strips humanity of its pretensions as well as endows it with vital purpose. Though tiny in the grand scheme of God's creative wonder, humanity's place is disproportionate to our size.

A living God cannot delight in the death of a marriage. What God has joined together, God will not lightly see taken apart. That much is clear in Jesus's stern words on divorce in Mark 10. What may be less clear, but no less important to realize, is that Jesus's opposition to divorce is a grace. God hates divorce because God loves people. Yet steady opposition to the reality of divorce does not exhaust God's grace. What God cannot condone, he willingly can forgive. That divine disposition for mercy is perhaps on keenest display in Jesus's welcoming of children. Drawing the most vulnerable into his arms of blessing, Christ commands his disciples to do the same.

Prayer of Inspiration

Lord, you are the great communicator. You speak through the wonders of the creation outside our windows and the marvel of the scriptures in our hands. And yet in these final days you speak most clearly through your Son, the Word made flesh. By your Holy Spirit, speak afresh today and in our encounter with the living Christ, cause us to listen. For we pray in Jesus's name. Amen.

Benediction

May the love of God the Father, who created you,

The grace of the Lord Jesus Christ, who redeemed you,

And the fellowship of the Holy Spirit who sanctifies you

Be with you all.

October 14, 2018

Passages: *Job 23:1-9, 16-17; Psalm 90:12-17; Hebrews 4:12-16; Mark 10:17-31*

Gathering Prayer

Eternal God, in this autumnal season we sense the passing of the years. Like the fall foliage, you paint our lives with beauty even as you remind us we shall each soon return to the earth from which we came. In this hour of worship, sanctify the time you give us. As we enter into the gift of these moments with you and your people, teach us to number our days aright. And in this encounter with the living Christ, form in us a heart of wisdom. For we pray in Jesus's name. Amen.

Preaching Theme

Job 23 is the voice of raw lament. Parched and anguished, it is a rhetoric refined by pain, distilled in the crucible of suffering to such a bitter proof that we wince with each sip. Awash in an ocean of grief, a cascade of suffering has knocked Job off his feet and now a riptide of poor counsel has kept him clawing for breath. Confronted with the horrific hiddenness of God, Job beats his knuckles bloody on the dark brass of heaven. Yet through it all, the darkness does not silence the voice of faith. Lament is a grammar of belief. It is the guttural "Why?" asked to the God who is listening. It is a sacred space that allows God to be God and grief to be grief, without needing to subsume the reality of one into the other. Like Psalm 139, Job 23 also reminds us that God is present in the darkness. There is no geography, physical or emotional, that lacks access to divinity. There is no journey to the east, west, north, or south that does not end in the presence of a watching and waiting God. Job 23 also points us to the gospel. The *Deus Absconditus*—the hidden God—is the very God we find revealed on the cross. For it is on the cross that Christ will take our lament to his lips and drink that distilled and bitter cup. To its very dregs.

Secondary Preaching Themes

Reminding us that the inexorable march of time has a melancholy cadence, Psalm 90 confronts us with the utter brevity and fragility of our temporal existence.

Human life, for all its pretensions and possibilities, is as inconsequentially finite as a tuft of desert grass drying in the sun even as it sprouts. Yet time's passing has a pedagogical purpose in verse 12. The turning of the years reminds us that we are temporary; only God is eternal. We are contingent; only God is constant. In that insight is freedom to live each day as a gift that cannot be grasped but that can be received in gratitude. That insight also grounds us in the hope of the gospel. For if the heart of wisdom is the realization that we are dying, even as we live, perhaps the heart of the gospel is that, in Christ, we live even as we die.

The lectionary's selection in Hebrews is classic bad news/good news. Hard on the heels of a bracing account of Israel's failure to enter God's rest, verses 12-13 present the word of God as a living and active double-edged sword slicing and dicing, cubing and cutting human souls until our very insides are laid bare before the burning eyes of a living God. Into that carnage of exposed sin steps our great high priest (vv. 14-16). Tempted and yet without sin, his body was carved and his soul laid bare on the cross for us. So the eyes that now watch from heaven beckon brightly to an open throne of grace (Heb 4:16).

We need to see that it was *after* "Jesus looked at him carefully *and loved him*" that Christ prescribed the hard medicine of selling all of the rich young man's possessions (Mark 10:21). Christ's call to complete dependence on him is not punitive; it is restorative. That is because the kingdom is something that can be received as a gift, not achieved as a trophy. We can enter only as dependent children, not independent oligarchs. That is why Jesus's famous image of a camel and needle drips with the hyperbole of grace. In ourselves we have no hope. In Christ we have it all.

Prayer of Application

God of the mountains and the valleys, we thank you that there is nowhere we can go where you are not. There is no journey we can take that will bring us outside the borders of your kingdom or the gaze of your eyes, or the reach of your love. Even in our far country of doubt and despair, remind us that you are near. For we pray in the name of our Immanuel, Jesus Christ. Amen.

Benediction

May the God who alone can graciously thread a camel through a needle,

so work in your heart and life,

that his blessings are woven through your days

with reminders that it is all grace. Amen.

October 21, 2018

Passages: *Job 38:1-7, 34-41; Psalm 91:9-16; Hebrews 5:1-10; Mark 10:35-45*

Gathering Prayer

Triune God, we see your power on display in the crackle of lightning and hear echoes of your image in the murmur of infants. As we gather today in a broken world still dappled with glimpses of your glory, quiet our questions and doubts enough to hear such reminders of your presence all around us. And in meeting with you, grant us the gift of trust. For we pray through Jesus. Amen.

Call to Worship (from Psalm 42)

Leader: Just like a deer that craves streams of water, my whole being craves you, God.

People: My whole being thirsts for God, for the living God.

Leader: My tears have been my food both day and night, as people constantly questioned me, "Where's your God now?"

People: Why, I ask myself, are you so depressed? Why are you so upset inside?

Leader: Hope in God!

People: Because I will again give him thanks, my saving presence and my God.

Preaching Theme

Thirst is a primordial craving; and the disciples felt it. Not a thirst for fluids but the deeper longing of parched human egos aching to be whetted with earthly glory. And so James and John come to Jesus asking him to endorse their blank check of ambition (Mark 10:35). Indulging their fancy, Jesus asks what they want. Their response reveals both the depth and direction of their desire: "Allow one of us to sit on your right and the other on your left when you enter your glory" (v. 37). They don't just want to sip on the Messiah's glory; they want to inhale it by the gulp.

Maybe that is why Jesus's response invokes a powerful image: "Can you drink the cup I drink…?" (v. 38). Behind that image is a deep biblical truth. The goblet the Messiah will take to his lips is not filled with the sweet wine of divine privilege, but is the bitter cup of God's wrath. That is why this episode is framed with a prediction of Jesus's suffering and death (Mark 10:32-34) and ends with one as well (v. 45). If the chosen beverage of the king is sacrifice, the way of the kingdom must also be marked by surrender. If the cup of the kingdom is redemptive suffering, the children of the king must follow their thirst in a new direction. The way to satisfy our yen for glory is not the way of ascendant power, but descendent service.

Secondary Preaching Themes

After over thirty chapters of divine silence echoing with the ache of humanity's question "Why?" in Job 38, God speaks from the whirlwind. Yet God's word is not one of consolation nor of explanation but of confrontation: "Who is this darkening counsel with words lacking knowledge?…I will interrogate you" (vv. 2-3). What follow are four full chapters of theodicy by safari. God takes Job from the bedrock of earth's foundation to the brilliance of the heavenly Pleiades, pausing to marvel at his own handiwork in hippos and lionesses. Amazingly, that was enough for Job (cf. chapter 42). Apparently in this zoo of grace, Job experienced not an explanation of the philosophical "why?" but a trust-inducing encounter with the personal "Who."

Psalm 91 is the patron psalm of all in danger. Yet it is hard to reconcile its soaring promises of absolute protection with the vicious and seemingly capricious meting out of suffering in a worn world. Perhaps a clarifying way to conceive of God's protection is not from individual instances of death, but from death's ultimate grip. The blow of the sword and pestilence still strikes, but the eternal sting is absent (1 Cor 15). We also are invited to see that our ultimate security was made possible by our Savior's vulnerability. In a world filled with sword and pestilence and danger, it was he who "was pierced because of our rebellions and crushed because of our crimes" so that "by his wounds" we may be healed.

In the opening ten verses of chapter 5, the author of Hebrews is wrestling to reconcile Jesus's high priesthood with his high Christology. How could Jesus be both the one who can deal gently with broken humanity (v. 2) as well as the mighty Son of God proclaimed in Psalm 2 (v. 5) and Psalm 110's eternal successor of Melchizedeck (v. 6)? The answer is the incarnation. It was "during his days on earth" (literally, "During the days of *his flesh*," v. 7) that "although he was a Son, he learned obedience from what he suffered" (v. 8). The incarnation is thus the guarantee that Jesus is the High Priest we need. He is the full Son of God in full solidarity with humanity.

Benediction

May the God who fashioned the world,

binds up the brokenhearted,

and promises to wipe the very tears from our eyes,

fill you with all joy and peace in faith

so that you overflow with hope by the power of the Holy Spirit.

October 28, 2018

Passages: Job 42:1-6, 10-17; Psalm 34:1-8 [19-22]; Hebrews 7:23-28; Mark 10:46-52

Call to Worship (based on Psalm 34)

Leader: I will bless the Lord at all times, his praise will always be in my mouth.

People: Magnify the Lord with me! Together let us lift his name up high!

Leader: I sought the Lord and he answered me. He delivered me from all my fears.

People: Magnify the Lord with me! Together let us lift his name up high!

Leader: Those who look to God will shine; their faces are never ashamed.

People: Magnify the Lord with me! Together let us lift his name up high!

Leader: On every side, the Lord's messenger protects those who honor God; and he delivers them.

People: Magnify the Lord with me! Together let us lift his name up high!

Leader: Taste and see how good the Lord is! The one who takes refuge in him is truly happy!

People: Magnify the Lord with me! Together let us lift his name up high!

Preaching Theme

Mark never misses a chance to show up Jesus's disciples, as he does in this story. A blind beggar calls out for Jesus's attention. If Jesus's response, "What do you want me to do for you?" sounds familiar, it's supposed to. Right before this story, Mark laid out another story—two of Jesus's disciples have a request for Jesus too. When they approach him, Jesus replies, "What do you want me to do for you?" The disciples ask to be seated alongside Jesus, to share his authority, to be important, to bask in his reflected glory.

But when Jesus asks a blind beggar, "What do you want me to do for you?" his request is far more simple: "Teacher, I want to see." And when Jesus heals the blind man, the result is that "he began to follow Jesus on the way." Blind, beggarly

Bartimaeus isn't looking to lead, but to follow. He isn't looking to be important but to do the most important thing—to see, to know, and to follow Christ.

In between these two contrasting requests comes Jesus's well-known teaching, "Whoever wants to be great among you will be your servant. Whoever wants to be first among you will be the slave of all, for the Human One didn't come to be served but rather to serve and to give his life to liberate many people." Is this what you want Jesus to do for you?

Secondary Preaching Themes

At a crude, unexamined level, many people relate to God as they might a genie in a bottle with three magic wishes in the offing. We go around asking God to do stuff for us—everything from primo parking to a radical cure for cancer. Some of our requests are silly and some very serious. But the request God, in Christ, delights to answer is to make us followers.

By the end of Job's saga, he demonstrates a humility appropriate to a creature in relation to the creator. His story is further evidence that blind Bartimaeus's approach to Jesus is much preferable to that of Jesus's disciples.

The story of Bartimaeus is set just before Jesus's entry into Jerusalem. While this story connects to the preceding story in terms of discipleship, it anticipates the coming story by demonstrating: 1) Jesus's interest in those others cast aside, 2) Jesus's ability to heal, a word used synonymously with "save" in these Gospel accounts, and 3) Jesus's focus on providing a way forward, a new life.

Prayer of Repentance

Lord God, creator of the universe, the stars in the sky and the coral in the sea belong to you. You are wonderful beyond our comprehension and yet we confess that we have tried to contain you in our books, in our theories, in our feelings, and our very best thoughts. Teach us the humility of Job that we might also pray, "I have indeed spoken about things I didn't understand, wonders beyond my comprehension." Keep surprising us, creator of the universe, and teach us humility and wonder at your presence, in your creation and among your people. Amen.

Invitation to Congregational Prayer

The book of Hebrews teaches us that Jesus, in whose name we pray, is "holy, innocent, incorrupt, separate from sinners, and raised high above the heavens" (7:26). Though he is so different from us, Jesus, in whose name we pray, holds us close. He is the one who "can completely save those who are approaching God through him, because he always lives to speak with God for them" (v. 25). Would you join me as we pray together in Jesus's name?

Who Is Calling Whom?

Mark 10:46-52

O. Wesley Allen, Jr.

I remember this one preacher from my childhood. It didn't matter what he was preaching on; some way or another he would work in the story of his call into the ministry. Talking about God creating the world in six days, he'd bring up his call. Talking about the Israelites being taken into exile, he'd fit in his call. Talking about the meaning of the Lord's Supper, he'd mention his call. Talking about the apocalyptic end of the world, he would slip in, "Reminds me of being in prison as a young man and sitting in cell 204 and giving my life to Jesus and starting to read the Bible and then God told me that when I got out I should go preach the word."

I'll bet every time he stood up to preach, God said, "I sure wish I had called the man in cell 205 instead!" I hated that story. Not just because he told it so often, but also because he made it sound like it was some special calling no one else experienced.

I've got to say over at the seminary, students constantly talk about their calling into ministry. I am pleased when they take the call to ministry seriously, but I am distressed as well. What bothers me is not how much we talk about calling around the seminary. It's how narrowly we talk about calling that I get tired of. A narrow understanding of God's calling goes against the Bible.

It goes against the story of the healing of Bartimaeus we just read. You see, the healing of Bartimaeus ain't your run-of-the-mill miracle. I know that sounds ridiculous, because a miracle, by its very definition, is something out of the ordinary. But compared with other miracle stories in the Gospels, this story does a lot more than just demonstrate Jesus's healing power. Of course, Mark's stories often have layers underneath layers of meaning. A surface layer of straightforward meaning, but underneath a layer of parabolic meaning. So on the surface, the Bartimaeus story is a healing story, but underneath it is a description of God's call offered to every Christian. To move to this deeper level, we need to think about Bartimaeus as much in terms of his being a beggar as we do in terms of his being blind. And we need to pay attention to the context in which Mark places the story of Bartimaeus the beggar.

As Jesus was going on the way, a man came up and asked him, "What must I do to obtain eternal life?" When Jesus told him that he should sell all he had, give it to the poor, and come and follow him, he went away sad because he had much.

Further on the way to Jerusalem, Jesus told his followers for a third time that he was going to be handed over and killed and after three days rise. At that point James and John came to Jesus and asked him for a blank-check sort of favor. Jesus asked them, "What do you want me to do for you?" They asked to be seated on Jesus's right and left when he came into his glory. When the other ten heard about the favor they requested, they became angry, and Jesus used the teaching moment to explain, again, that to be a follower of Jesus is to be a servant. And he reminded them that he was himself a model of such servanthood, saying, "For the Human One didn't come to be served but rather to serve and to give his life to liberate many people."

And then Jesus and his followers came to Jericho. And there Bartimaeus sat on the side of the way on the edge of Jericho. He is forced to beg because there are no vocational centers to train people with disabilities in the ancient Roman Empire, especially in occupied lands such as Palestine. But as far as begging goes, just before Passover is as good a season as it gets, because lots of pilgrims on the way to Jerusalem for the festival have to come right through Jericho. So, for the moment, business is pretty good.

As people pass by on the way out of the city, he would call out to them hoping they would throw a coin or two into his cloak—in those days beggars spread out their cloaks the way street musicians today open their guitar cases in front of them as they play. "Have mercy on me. Have mercy on a poor beggar." Some would pitch a little spare change into his cloak. Others would ignore him. And still others would chastise him, "Be quiet. Get a job. Quit pestering people."

There he sits on the side of the way that heads out of Jericho, doing his usual rap, when he hears that Jesus of Nazareth is in the crowd passing by. So like any beggar who knows how to get the most out of a situation, Bartimaeus narrows his attention from the crowd in general to Jesus in particular. "Son of David, Jesus, have mercy on me.... C'mon, brother, can you spare a dime?" Some try to rebuke him into silence. But you don't miss the chance to play the palace, so he yells out even louder, "Son of David, have mercy on me."

And he successfully gets Jesus's attention. Jesus has him called over. Odd isn't it—to call a blind man to you instead of you going over to him? But Bartimaeus comes. And when he comes, he does something even odder. He throws his cloak aside and leaves it behind. That's like a blind beggar, in today's stereotype, throwing away his tin cup just before he's about to make his best pitch.

It's no wonder then that Jesus asks Bartimaeus what he wants from him. That may seem awfully insensitive for a healer to ask a blind man, "What do you want me to do for you?" But it's a perfectly natural question for a potential donor to ask a beggar who has just thrown away his cloak. And this perfectly natural question opens the door for Bartimaeus to make the most important beg of his life: "Rabbouni, let me receive my sight."

And Jesus gives him what he asks for and says, "Your faith has healed you." Well, actually, he doesn't just say, "Your faith has healed you." He adds, "Go, your faith has healed you." *Go?* Jesus didn't do anything for this blind beggar on the side of the way until Bartimaeus called out to him. And now, in the same breath that he heals him, he sends him away. "Go, your faith has healed you."

Well, indeed, the gift of sight is also the gift of mobility. Bartimaeus now has the freedom to go that he did not have before. Bartimaeus is no longer limited to going only where someone is willing to lead him. He now has the freedom to choose his own path. So what does he do with the mobility, with the new freedom that his sight gives him? Where does he go? He follows Jesus on the way. He takes up the path of a disciple. In other words, he is finally given the freedom to go anywhere he wants, and he chooses to allow himself to be led around again. And this time he is being led by one who is on the way to Golgotha.

This is a call story. It has all of the elements of more explicit call stories. I mean, Bartimaeus casts aside his livelihood, meager though it may be, to follow Jesus. And because Jesus is just about to enter Jerusalem, we get the sense that Bartimaeus personifies the call to deny yourself, take up your cross, and follow Jesus. This passage has all of the elements of a call story. Well, all of the elements except one minor thing. *Bartimaeus is never called!* The fishermen are ordered to follow. The tax collector is commanded to follow. The rich man is invited to follow. But Bartimaeus is told to *go*.

He is never explicitly called to discipleship, but he claims it as his path. He accepts a calling that is never made to him, but was his for the taking nevertheless.

We talk about calling in the church all the time, and I respect those of you who respond to that call by gathering here each week to worship and work for the Lord. But I am in awe of the Bartimaeuses out there who follow on the path of discipleship without others recognizing that they are called. As a late-thirties, white, middle-class, heterosexual, American, Protestant male, I am inspired by those who do not share the privilege of race, birth place, gender, age, education, sexual orientation, and economic status, who have heard the word "Go" spoken at them so many times that they begin to think it is their middle name, but who nevertheless deny themselves, take up their crosses, and follow Christ on the way as he offers his life as a ransom for many. I am moved by those who say, "*I have not been called but, by God, I should be!*"

When I was in seminary, there was a professor visiting the Divinity School who was on sabbatical from the university where he taught English literature. We became close and he told me how as a young boy he would play the piano at Southern Baptist revivals where his father would preach. I asked him, "Here you are, an English professor, taking courses at a seminary during your sabbatical. Have you ever felt called into ministry?" He told me he had always wanted to be called, but never really was. As he grew up he felt rejected by both his father and his denomination, because he was gay. He eventually found a home in the Episcopal Church, but he still never felt called by the church. And he told me, "If they don't want me to come in through the front door, I'll sneak in through the back." And sure enough, he gave as much of his time, intellect, and energy to the church as anyone I've ever known. He read scripture and served as a chalice bearer in worship any time he got the chance. He accepted a number of lay offices in running the parish. And when the church began a Stephen's Ministry program, he jumped in with all his might. He began caring for the sick, visiting the shut-ins, counseling with the troubled. And then he began training others, both people in his parish and in the national program. I am in awe when I stand before people who take up the role of radical discipleship without being clearly called to do so.

When I was nineteen and in college, I began serving a small rural church whose pastor had become ill. That summer I attended licensing school, a requirement so that I could administer the sacraments as well as get a little training in preaching, pastoral care, church administration, and so forth. On the last day of the two-week-long school, it was announced that we had to take a literacy test. There was an older man there who said, "I don't know why I need to know how to read and write. I'm going to be preaching." I thought to myself, *I cannot believe this is the kind of person the United Methodist Church is appointing in the pastorate.* A little later I overheard the leaders expressing frustration over this fellow's ability, or lack of ability, when one of them said, "I don't know what to do with him. Do you know he has already sold his home and quit his job because he thinks the bishop should send him to a church even though he has been warned he might not get an appointment?" Now I don't know whether that man was qualified to be a pastor or not, but I have always been in awe of the fact that he demanded to be called.

Argentina in the 1970s was a place where brutal dictatorship was torturing and killing many of its own citizens, and anyone who was critical of the government or chose to work with the poor and suffering masses was in danger of becoming one of the "Disappeared Ones." You have probably heard of the small group of Argentinian women who felt they could no longer be silent. No one called them. Indeed, as they went into government office after government office asking for information on disappeared loved ones, they were told, "Go." As they asked church after church to help them, they were told, "Go." Finally, they decided to do just that, to go—to go into the streets on a Thursday afternoon at five o'clock and hold a silent hour vigil around the Plaza de Mayo in front of the government buildings. Protests against the government were a capital offense. Probably because they were seen as having no real power as women, the government ignored them as they walked around with pictures of lost loved ones hanging from their necks. One of the women did eventually disappear, probably as a warning to all the others. But it was too late. Within weeks the number of women keeping the weekly vigil had swelled into the hundreds and within months into the thousands. They came to be known as the Mothers of the Plaza de Mayo, and women from around the world joined in solidarity with them by sending money, by lobbying their own governments, and by coming and joining in the vigils. These women, silenced and ignored, were instrumental in the downfall of a dictatorship and in the return of democracy to Argentina. They were told they were not called, they were sent away, but they nevertheless denied themselves, took up their crosses, and followed on the way that led to Jerusalem.

Would that those of us who have heard the words "*Come, follow me*" do so well as those who have heard the word "*Go*"! I am in awe of the faith that has saved the Bartimaeuses of the world! I long for that faith.

November 4, 2018

Passages: Ruth 1:1-8; Psalm 119:1-8; Hebrews 9:11-14; Mark 12:28-34

Preaching Theme

The book of Ruth is a simple story on the surface, but don't stay there. Dig deep and you'll be rewarded with paradoxes, turnarounds, and the unexpected delight of a God who does not give up on us, even when we have given up on both God and ourselves.

"Bethlehem" means "place of bread," so already in verse 1 we see we are in for a bumpy ride. The "place of bread" is in famine. Seeking a new life, Naomi's husband and two sons meet death instead but not before providing Naomi with two Moabite daughters-in-law. A poor widow with no children might plead for companionship and company on a lonely journey home. Instead she pushes them away. She wants what is best for them and not for herself.

But don't stop where the lectionary reading ends! Note that these Moabite women who have everything to lose by becoming aliens and strangers in Naomi's homeland, hold on to her for dear life. In fact, Ruth will not be dissuaded in her loyalty. Toward the end of chapter 1, Naomi names her plight by renaming herself. She says, "Don't call me Naomi [meaning pleasant], but call me Mara [meaning bitter], for the Almighty has made me very bitter. I went away full, but the LORD has returned me empty" (vv. 20-21).

Spoiler alert: Naomi will be singing a far different tune—a lullaby—by the time this story is over. "Could the world be about to turn?"

Secondary Preaching Themes

"The Canticle of the Turning," otherwise named "My Soul Cries Out with a Joyful Shout," is a robust hymn to add in almost any congregational context. Based on the Magnificat, you could learn it now and use it through Advent. This song compellingly captures the tension Naomi raises in the book of Ruth. It is a tension that haunts God's people in scripture, history, and your church's pews—longing for a day when all things will be set right. The refrain holds out this hope: "My heart shall sing of the day you bring. Let the fires of your justice burn. Wipe away all tears, for the dawn draws near, and the world is about to turn!"

Naomi's hope remains unfulfilled at the end of chapter 1, but Ruth is our clue that something of God's redemption might still belong to this story. Similarly, you know the hopes of a congregation that files in for worship and you know how many remain unfulfilled. In Hebrews 9 Jesus is the fulfillment of the Hebrew sacrificial system. Using what the congregation already knows, the preacher in Hebrews fills the listening audience with unexpected delight. "He passed through the greater and more perfect meeting tent, which isn't made by human hands.... He entered the holy of holies once for all by his own blood, not by the blood of goats or calves, securing our deliverance for all time...how much more will the blood of Jesus wash our consciences clean from dead works in order to serve the living God?" (vv. 11-12, 14). The God who will finally turn the world to rights has already begun this work in Jesus Christ, our clue that something of God's redemption might still belong in our stories.

Invitation to and Prayer of Confession (based on Psalm 119:1-8)

L: Those whose way is blameless—

       who walk in the Lord's instruction—are truly happy!

       Those who guard God's laws are truly happy!

       They seek God with all their hearts.

       They don't even do anything wrong!

       They walk in God's ways.

       Let us confess our sin together:

       God, you have ordered that your decrees

       should be kept most carefully.

P: **How I wish my ways were strong**

       when it comes to keeping your statutes!

       Then I wouldn't be ashamed

       when I examine all your commandments.

       I will give thanks to you with a heart that does right

       as I learn your righteous rules.

       I will keep your statutes.

       Please don't leave me all alone!

Assurance of Pardon

Hebrews 9 tells us that, in Jesus Christ, our consciences are washed clean from dead works in order to serve a living God. Jesus Christ offered himself to God through the eternal Spirit as a sacrifice without any flaw. In him we are forgiven.

Sending Litany

L: Hear these words of Jesus when someone asked him, "Which commandment is the most important of all?" He replied—

P: "The most important commandment is Israel, listen! Our God is the one Lord, and you must love the Lord your God with all your heart, with all your being, with all your mind, and with all your strength. The second is this, You will love your neighbor as yourself. No other commandment is greater than these."

L: Indeed, friends, when we live and believe these words, Jesus himself assures us: "You aren't far from God's kingdom." Go in peace to love God and neighbor!

November 11, 2018

Passages: *Ruth 3:1-5; 4:13-17; Psalm 146; Hebrews 9:24-28; Mark 12:38-44*

Preaching Theme

During family movie nights, my parents would often fast-forward through the parts of our main feature that were not suitable for my young eyes. In this week's lectionary selections from Ruth, we see a similar phenomenon. Naomi tells Ruth to pursue Boaz for a husband. Ruth dutifully agrees. Fast-forward to the part where Ruth and Boaz are married and Naomi, who was once bereft of family, now has her arms full of baby! But don't you want to know what happens in the middle?

Ruth's move is bold to say the least. In modern terms, Boaz is away on business, celebrating a big acquisition. He has spent the evening eating and boozing with his buddies on the company credit card. Boaz stumbles back to the hotel, looks up from fumbling for his key, and sees Ruth leaning against the doorframe of his hotel room, waiting for him. He pushes her into the room in case one of their colleagues sees her and starts the office gossip chain a'rattling.

What we know of Boaz is nothing but integrity and he sets out to make an honest woman out of Ruth. He protects Ruth's reputation, handles the complicated legalities, likely sacrificing some of his own financial advantage, and makes good his promise to redeem all that was lost for Naomi.

In Boaz's actions, we see the restoration of what was lost, the filling up of what was empty, the sweetening of bitter waters. In Boaz's actions, we begin to imagine a redeemer who might do the same for us—restore what is lost, fill up what is empty, sweeten our own bitter hearts. In admiration of Boaz, we begin to admire the one who is coming, a redeemer who is kinsman to us all.

Secondary Preaching Themes

Today is a holiday in much of the Western world. Remembrance Day in the United Kingdom or Canada, Veterans Day in the United States. It can be difficult to bring patriotic holidays into the sanctuary, but this morning's psalm helps us do it. Early on, World War I was called "The War to End All Wars." However, the "I" after World War reminds us that there was another war that followed close in its wake. Perhaps it is a misnomer altogether that war can end war, that violence can end violence. That is why the psalmist says, "Don't trust leaders; don't trust any human beings—there's no saving help with them!" (v. 3). Turn instead to "the LORD." He is the only one who can save, who can redeem, who can bring peace and restoration where there is war and violence.

While Psalm 146 looks forward to this redemption, Hebrews 9 tells us how it works and puts it in the present tense. Jesus Christ is our Boaz. Jesus Christ is the Lord who rules forever!

Invitation to Confession

When Jesus wants to hold up an example of sin, he doesn't point to the outskirts or to the margins of polite, even pious, society. He points directly into the middle of the temple or, if he were standing here today, points directly into the middle of this sanctuary, saying, "Watch out for the legal experts. They like to walk around in long robes. They want to be greeted with honor in the markets. They long for places of honor in the synagogues and at banquets. They are the ones who cheat widows out of their homes, and to show off they say long prayers. They will be judged most harshly."

Knowing our guilt, let us confess our sins to the only one who might forgive us and grant us grace to try again.

Assurance of Pardon

For what we have done and for what we have left undone, scripture is clear that the penalty of sin is death. But God, in creative and abundant mercy, bore that death for us so that we might live. As Hebrews 9 tells us, "People are destined to die once and then face judgment. In the same way, Christ was also offered once to take on himself the sins of many people. He will appear a second time, not to take away sin but to save those who are eagerly waiting for him" (vv. 27-28). In Christ there is forgiveness and abundant hope of salvation and new life. In him we are forgiven!

Introduction to the Offering

When Jesus wants to hold up an example of righteousness to his disciples, he does not look to the wealthy or the powerful. He observes a widow—poor and powerless in that society— who doesn't give much but who gives it in an extravagance of love. Calling the disciples around him, he holds her up in comparison to other givers, saying, "All of them are giving out of their spare change. But she from her hopeless poverty has given everything she had, even what she needed to live on" (Mark 12:44). We needn't give much, but now we have opportunity to give in an extravagance of love.

November 18, 2018

Passages: 1 Samuel 1:14-20; Psalm 16; Hebrews 10:11-14 (15-18), 19-25; Mark 13:1-8

Gathering Prayer (based on Psalm 16)

Protect us, O God, as we gather. In this sanctuary, we take our refuge in you. You alone are God, apart from you we have no good thing. You have not abandoned us but have brought us here to learn the way of life. In your presence is total celebration and beautiful things come to us from your right hand. Let us bless the Lord together! Hallelujah, Amen!

Preaching Theme

If you've ever learned a new game—a sport, video game, or board game—you've likely started with two questions: "How does this end?" and "What am I supposed to do until then?" The author/preacher of the book of Hebrews regularly circles back to the readers/hearers with answers to these questions. In this morning's epistle lesson, the answer to the first question is that Jesus wins! Other priests have to make their sacrifices over and over again. But Jesus, by the one sacrifice of his perfect and holy life, takes away the sin of the world. He reigns with God and now waits until all his enemies come in submission to his rule. And because Jesus wins, we are assured the outcome as well: Jesus "perfected the people who are being made holy with one offering for all time" (Heb 1:14).

Ah, but that's the tricky part. We know how it ends…but it isn't over yet. "The people who are being made holy" still have work to do. The author/preacher of Hebrews has something to say about that. Because of all that has already been accomplished by Christ, we are to have hope in various forms. A God-given hope that fills us with sustaining faith. A God-given hope that we needn't stand condemned any longer. A God-given hope that we might be useful to one another in the meantime. This is not a hope that wanes as the game moves on; rather this is hope that eagerly awaits Christ who has set the path for victory. We live in God-given hope until Christ comes again in victory, acknowledged by all as champion and king.

Secondary Preaching Themes

Hannah, who fervently prays in the temple, is a wonderful example of hope restored. Eli, who is only human himself as evidenced by the fact that he can't tell the difference between drunkenness and fervent prayer, is an example of the faithful priesthood, standing "every day serving and offering the same sacrifices over and over, sacrifices that can never take away sins" (Heb 10:11). If Eli, though bound by human weakness, can offer such great hope, how much more can we look forward to Christ as our Great High Priest? If Hannah finds such joy and hope in the birth of a son, how much more can we see Christ—himself the product of miraculous birth—as the answer to all our most fervent prayers?

It can be tempting to read Mark 13, as many have done, with great gloom and foreboding. Everyone break out your placards and dire prognostications, "The end is near!" An alternate translation of the Greek word *telos*, translated in this text as "end," might also be "completion, perfection, or purpose." The perfection and purpose of Christ's kingdom is not chaos. It is not earthquakes and famine and war. These things are not the end! Rather, they remind us that Christ's kingdom will be completed someday by Christ himself. And these things remind us that great patience is needed in God's world and provided in Christ's sacrifice.

Prayer of Repentance

God of Truth, we confess that we are easily deceived by shiny things and outlandish promises. We like for things to be easy, for our categories to be tidy, and there are preachers, programs, and products galore that cater to these false hopes.

God of Peace, we confess that we are easily frightened by wars and rumors of wars. Nations rage, gangs protect their territory, politicians draw up lines, even churches and families are not immune from violence and abuse. In our fear, we build walls and defenses.

God of Creation, tectonic plates shift, drought and famine affect the most vulnerable among us. Help us, God of Truth, Peace, and Creation, to know that brokenness is not the end of the story. Forgive our waywardness and fear. Remind us that you are in control, you are working still, and we can trust in you always. In Jesus's name, Amen.

Sending Forth (based on Psalm 16)

Go out into the world with assurance that the Lord is your portion and your cup.

We will bless the Lord.

The Lord knows your past and your future and will never abandon you.

We will bless the Lord

The Lord is always before you and you will not stumble.

We will bless the Lord

In the Lord's presence is total celebration. Beautiful things come from God's right hand.

We will bless the Lord.

Go in peace to love and to serve!

November 25, 2018–Christ the King Sunday

Passages: 2 Samuel 23:1-7; Psalm 93; Revelation 1:4b-8; John 18:33-37

Opening Litany of Praise (based on Psalm 93 and Article 1 of "Our World Belongs to God"[1])

The Lord rules!

He is robed in majesty

And clothed with strength.

In a world that some seek to control

And others view with despair,

We joyfully declare:

He set the world firmly in place;

it won't be shaken.

His throne lasts forever.

Only he is eternal!

Though evil surrounds us

And chaos threatens to wash over us like a mighty river

We do not lose heart.

For the Lord is mightier than the sound of much water;

He is mightier than the sea's waves.

Mighty on high is the Lord!

Preaching Theme

There is a scene in *The Wizard of Oz* in which Dorothy and her friends have finally gained an audience with the legendary Wizard. Smoke fills the air, his voice booms around them, and the four friends quake with fear—until Dorothy's little dog Toto slips away, pulls back a curtain, and exposes the real Oz. That is when Dorothy and her friends discover that things are not how they first appeared. The great and powerful Oz is not so great and powerful after all.

Something similar happens in Revelation 1. Only this time, when the curtain is pulled back, the situation is reversed. With an oppressive emperor sitting on the throne in Rome and persecution breaking out all around them, John's congregations may well have wondered if Jesus Christ was so great and powerful after all. It is chaos, not Jesus, that appears to rule their world. Yet Revelation 1 insists that things are not how they appear. When the curtain is pulled back, Jesus Christ is not only revealed to be the one who *will be* the ruler of the kings of the earth. No. He is spoken of as the one who *is* the ruler of the kings of the earth (v. 5). Despite how things may first appear, his power and reign are a present reality. John drives this point home in verses 4 and 7, where he twice insists that the Lord God is the one who *is* and was and will be (note how John breaks the expected sequence of past/present/future in order to place the present tense in the emphatic position). The "isness" of God's presence and Christ's reign are what the church celebrates on Christ the King Sunday. Yes, someday every eye will see him coming on the clouds (v. 7). But those who have the eyes of faith can see that Lord God is with us—today. Jesus is king—today. So he deserves our worship and allegiance—today.

Secondary Preaching Themes

John 18:33-37

"Is Jesus really the king?" It was Pilate's question in John 18. But it is ours too. In a world that seems to be constantly falling apart (despite Psalm 93's insistence that the King of kings has set it firmly in its place), it can be hard to believe that Jesus is really the king. Yet he is. But as Jesus reminds us in John 18, he is a different kind of king. Sometimes, he chooses to clothe himself in weakness instead of strength. Sometimes, he robes himself in meekness instead of majesty (Ps 93:1). Sometimes, he comes as the king of the cross instead of the king of glory.

2 Samuel 23:1-7

North Americans seem quick to blame their politicians when things go wrong but slow to give them credit when things go right. King David knew better. In 2 Samuel 23:3-4, he uses soaring poetry to celebrate the difference a good king can make and to declare that another king (an even greater king than him!) is coming. David declares that it will happen. And thanks be to God, in Jesus Christ, it has.

Illustration: Some years ago, Allstate Insurance ran a popular advertising campaign featuring a character named "Mayhem." In each ad, Mayhem takes on a new form (a satellite dish, a texting teenager, or a poorly secured Christmas tree) to wreak havoc on the unsuspecting. After each incident, an ominous voice says, "Mayhem is everywhere...are you in good hands?" In a world full of mayhem, God's people may come into worship this week wondering if they are in good hands. May they leave with the assurance that they are because Jesus is king.

Prayer of Application

Almighty and ever-present God, by your Spirit, open the eyes of our hearts so that we might see, even through the veil of our tears, that you are the King of kings and Lord of lords. Assure us that, in Jesus Christ, you are for us, and not against us. May his victory over sin and death fill us with hope, patience, and perseverance and inspire us to prayer as we look forward to the coming of your kingdom in all its fullness. In the name of Jesus Christ, our present and coming king we pray, Amen.

Sending Words

Jesus Christ is king! He has defeated the powers of sin and death. He is the ruler of the kings of the earth. He loves us and has freed us from our sins by his blood. Therefore, wherever we go this week, whatever we do, may we give our full allegiance to him!

December 2, 2018–First Sunday of Advent

Passages: Jeremiah 33:14-16; Psalm 25:1-10; 1 Thessalonians 3:9-13; Luke 21:25-36

Opening Prayer

Faithful God:

As we gather to worship on this first Sunday of Advent:

Give us hearts that are open to hope.

Give us feet that stand firm on your promises.

Give us eyes that are alert to the ways you come among us.

Give us hands that are ready to work for your kingdom.

In the name of Jesus, our coming king we pray,

Amen.

Preaching Theme

The events Jesus describes in Luke 21 would be enough to make even the bravest souls run for cover. This chapter is "full of emergency...it's a whole drum roll of disaster."[1] Seas surge. Planets shake. The earth groans and threatens to come undone. The world Jesus describes is full of events both terrible and terrifying. In other words, the world Jesus describes is not unlike our own. Wars? We've got those. Persecutions? Yep. We've got those too. Natural disasters? Have you visited CNN.com lately? Jesus's predictions seem to be ripped right from the latest headlines.

Are these terrible events a sign that the end is indeed near? Are they an indication that Jesus might come, in all his power and glory, next Tuesday afternoon? Perhaps. But perhaps such speculation misses the point. Perhaps the point is that it always feels like the end of the world somewhere. That somewhere might be in an AIDS-stricken village in Kenya or in the bombed-out streets of Syria. But that somewhere might also be in the heart of the person in the pew who was laid off last week, or who was recently diagnosed with multiple sclerosis, or who is facing their first Christmas alone. All these things can feel like the end of the world and can make us want to run for cover, to cower in a corner and quiver with fear. Yet Jesus insists that we need not be afraid. Instead, when things seem to be going from bad to worse to worse again, Jesus invites us to stand tall, to lift up our heads, and to strain our eyes toward the horizon because it is precisely at such desperate moments that he promises to come. He may not come to us today as he will one day—riding on the clouds, with all his power and glory on full display. But by his Spirit, he still promises to come. And that is good news for today—even if the world does not end tomorrow!

Secondary Preaching Themes

Patience may be a virtue. But it is not one most of us want to cultivate. Instead, we download apps on our phones that let us skip the line at Starbucks, pay for Amazon Prime subscriptions that entitle us to quick delivery of our latest purchases, and spend our Friday nights watching whatever is available on Netflix Instant. We do not like to wait for coffee or a slow Internet connection. And we do not like to wait for God. As Anne Lamott observes, believing in God is easy. It is waiting on him that is hard.[2] Psalm 25 and Jeremiah 33 come as encouragement to those who are tired of waiting for God and who may be ready to give up. These texts assure us that the one for whom we wait is faithful. Because he kept the promise he made through the prophet Jeremiah in Christ's first advent, we can trust that he has not forgotten us, but will remember us according to his unfailing love (Ps 25:7).

Lewis Smedes once wrote that the greatest challenge for people who believe in the Christ's second coming is to live "the sort of life that makes people say, 'Ah, so that's how people are going to live when righteousness takes over our world.'"[3] Psalm 25 and 1 Thessalonians 3 exhort God's people to do exactly that, while assuring them that such a life is not ultimately a result of their own striving, but is the gift of the one who makes us "blameless in holiness," promises to "increase and enrich [our] love" (1 Thess 3:12-13), and is able to lead us in paths that are "loving and faithful" (Ps 25:10).

Prayer of Confession (based on Psalm 25:1-10)

Gracious God:

As we wait and watch for your coming among us,

Show us how we should live.

Make your ways known to me, Lord; teach me your paths.

Lead me in your truth.

Lord, remember your compassion and faithful love—they are forever.

But don't remember the sins of my youth or my wrongdoing.

(Time of silent confession)

The Lord is good and does the right thing;

The Lord teaches sinners which way they should go.

All his paths are loving and faithful.

The Lord remembers us only according to his faithful love.

The Lord remembers us in Jesus Christ!

Those who put their hope in him will not be put to shame!

Parting Blessing (based on 1 Thessalonians 3:12-13)

May the Lord cause your love to increase and overflow.

May the Lord cause your hearts to be strengthened with his hope and peace,

And may the Lord keep you blameless in holiness until he comes again.

Amen.

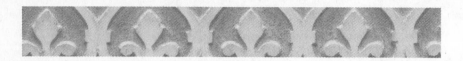

December 9, 2018–Second Sunday of Advent

Passages: Malachi 3:1-4; Luke 1:68-79; Philippians 1:3-11; Luke 3:1-6

Call to Worship (based on Luke 1:68-75)

Bless the Lord because he has come to help and has delivered his people.

Prepare the way for the Lord!

He has raised up a mighty Savior for us in his servant David's house,

just as he said through the mouths of his prophets long ago.

Prepare the way for the Lord!

He has brought salvation from our enemies

and from the power of all those who hate us.

Prepare the way for the Lord!

He has shown the mercy promised to our ancestors,

and remembered his holy covenant

so that we could serve him without fear.

Prepare the way for the Lord!

Prayer for Illumination

Refining God:

As we open your Word, open us to your voice.

Give us the courage to listen when you challenge us,

Give us the strength to follow where you lead us.

May your Spirit work in us

So that we will not go away from this place unchanged.

We pray this in the name of your Son, who redeems us

And by the power of your Spirit, who purifies us.

Amen.

Preaching Theme

What must you do to prepare for Christmas? Drag the tree out of the basement? Bake a few dozen cookies? Get your shopping done? The to-do list may already be long. But John the Baptist, whose chief job is to help God's people prepare for the coming of Jesus (Mal 3:1; Luke 1:76), insists that our lists must include one more thing. John says that if we want to be prepared for Christmas and for the coming of the king, we must *repent* (Luke 3:3).

Repentance is not a word we relish. Perhaps that is because it brings to mind embarrassing images of wild-eyed street corner preachers barking hellfire through their megaphones. But maybe our real problem with repentance runs deeper. To "repent" means to change. It involves identifying a sinful behavior or pattern, stopping it, and replacing it with something new. In this way, repentance is very simple. But it is also very hard because most of us do not want to change. Therefore, we prefer remorse to repentance. As Barbara Brown Taylor observes, "We would rather say, 'I'm sorry, I'm so sorry, I feel really, really awful about what I have done' than actually start doing things differently…our chronic guilt is the price we are willing to pay in order to avoid changes."[4]

Repentance is not easy, but John will not settle for anything less. That may come as hard news during a season when we just want to experience a little Christmas cheer. But in the end, John is not out to squelch our joy. Instead, he is out to help us find it by preparing us to receive the greatest gift the world has ever been given—the gift of Jesus Christ.

Secondary Preaching Themes

"I am not good enough for church…I've got to clean my act up first." Every pastor has heard some version of this speech. If you only read John's sermon in Luke 3 this week, you might get the impression that it is spot on! However, the additional lectionary assignments help to provide a more nuanced picture. These texts make clear that repentance is not something we do alone. Instead, it is something that God does in us and alongside of us (Phil 1:6; Mal 3:2-3). Furthermore, while the scrubbing and scouring Malachi anticipates may make us want to run for cover like children at bath time, these texts also assure us that God's intent is not to reject us or harm us, but to redeem and restore us so that we can live without fear in his presence forever (Luke 1:74).

Illustration: In one of his sermons,[5] Craig Barnes recalls watching a friend from China hand out gifts at a Christmas party some years ago. As the young man made his way around the room, Barnes noticed that whenever he passed someone a gift, he always used two hands. When asked about the practice, the young man explained, "We always give and receive gifts with two hands because for a moment we share the present, *not hiding or withholding anything.*" Our God is a two-handed giver. He does not withhold anything—not even his own Son. However God's incredible gift is not only given "with two hands," it must also be received "with two hands." This is where repentance comes in. Repentance is the way we lay down our sins so that our hands might be open to receive the incredible gift that God has given us in Jesus Christ.

Sending (from Philippians 1 and Malachi 3)

May your love become rich,

May you be refined like gold and silver

And may you be filled with the fruit of righteousness.

This is the gift of Jesus Christ!

May you serve him without fear and be found without blame on the day he comes again.

He will be faithful and finish his work in us!

To him be glory and praise forever and ever! **Amen!**

The Shrill One

Luke 3:1-20

Scott Hoezee

John was on a roll. For quite some time he had been preaching a fiery message to all kinds of people and with splendid results. They came to him in droves and responded to his message with genuine fervor. That is quite amazing given that John was not exactly what anyone would consider "seeker-friendly." Today most churches want to enfold visitors, give them a warm greeting. But that wasn't John the Baptist's style! He had too much fire in his belly to bother with what he might have deemed social pleasantries.

When people came to him, John was not adverse to sneering. "Well, well, well, here you all are trotting out to see me, but do you know what you look like to me? A bunch of slithering snakes fleeing a burning field! Who told you the fire was coming up behind you? What brings you here anyway?" Probably not a few folks blanched at such a greeting! Maybe some of them started to say something like, "Now just hold on there a moment, John. We're not pagans, you know. We're devout Jews, Abraham's children, heirs of the covenant. You can't talk that way to us! Save that for the Greeks and Romans!"

But before they could get very far, John cut them off. "Hush up! I've had it up to here listening to talk of 'Abraham's children, Abraham's children!' God isn't interested in your family tree but wants you to be a *living* tree of faith right now, producing spiritual fruit. If God wanted motionless, nonproductive people, he could create them out of these rocks. You people are not living examples of faith but are more like marble statues, monuments to bygone people of faith but dead as stone yourselves!"

Now you might think that this would be such a huge turnoff that folks would flee and head back home. But mostly that didn't happen. John was so fiercely effective that before the people even knew what they were doing, they blurted out, "What should we do!?" John got through to them. He shook up not just untutored peasants but also tax collectors, well-to-do folks, and even strapping Roman soldiers. Think of that: John made armed men with shields and helmets quiver like scared children.

In every case, when anyone asked John for advice on how to live better lives, John always came up with an answer. He encouraged generosity, honesty, fairness. He told tax collectors not to cook the books so as to line their own pockets. He told soldiers to stop shaking people down and coercing bribes. Basically John told the people to be nice, to tell the truth, to share.

Who knows what the people thought he was going to say. Perhaps they anticipated some heavy-duty admonitions to do spectacular ministry like opening a leprosy clinic or establishing a relief agency for victims of famine. But no, John's advice was far simpler. Some years ago many of us looked at that book *All I Ever Need to Know I Learned in Kindergarten*. It was a pretty simple little book, almost trite in one way. Yet it sold well because it made a very good point: if we could just find grown-up ways to live out the kindergarten virtues of kindness and sharing, the world would be a better place. So also with John the Baptist. The people expected John to give them graduate school–like spiritual direction so they could all earn their religious PhDs, but instead John took them back to kindergarten. John didn't promote spiritual PhDs but spiritual ABCs.

And it worked. John was on a roll. It's difficult to know just what was going through John's mind as his ministry progressed. But if he felt good about the way God was using him, if his confidence level was rising steadily as time went by, you could hardly blame him. It's not that John was getting cocky, but he had hit on a formula that was working. So the day came when John dared to take on even Herod. Luke is sketchy as to how this came about, but clearly at some point John condemned Herod for his moral failings, chief among which was marrying his sister-in-law.

And it was precisely here that John's roll came to an end. Now he had gone too far. This time John criticized someone who was *not* going to be cut to the quick. This time he upset the wrong man and so suddenly found himself under arrest and locked up in a prison where he would remain until the end of his days.

But that last verse is not Herod's first appearance in Luke 3, is it? If you ever have to read scripture in church, then Luke 3:1 is the kind of passage you hope you never get. For the second chapter in a row, Luke opens with a litany of then-current political leaders. But at least with Luke 2 we have the advantage of having heard "Quirinius" pronounced at any number of Sunday school Christmas programs over the years. Luke 3 is far less familiar, throwing in names like "Traconitis" and "Lysanius" among others. All in all, it's a pretty elaborate historical setup. But if it at first seemed unnecessary, by the time you hit verses 19-20, you realize Luke included all those political names for a reason. He wasn't merely fixing the date of John the Baptist's ministry.

If I tell you that a certain event took place "while Richard Nixon was president," then you know that whatever I'm talking about happened somewhere between 1969 and 1974. So also in Luke 3, once Luke mentions all those names, from Tiberius Caesar on down, anyone familiar with Roman history would know when John's ministry happened. But this nod toward that era's political leaders was more than just a historical footnote. It is Luke's way of reminding us that the gospel is not an isolated phenomenon that takes place off in some corner. The gospel is not a local reality but is cosmic.

Luke also quotes for us a few verses from Isaiah. But notice that this prophecy does not say that *some* valleys will be filled in and just a *few* mountains would be made low. He doesn't in the end say that a handful of people would see the salvation of God. No, he says *every* valley, *every* mountain, and *all* of humanity would be involved. *All* the crooked roads would be made straight and *all* the rough places would be smoothed out.

So if someone had said to John, "Don't concern yourself with Herod. He's too far away to bother with," you sense that John would have been furious. He was not called by God to put on a cute little sideshow restricted to the banks of the Jordan River. John's job was to prepare *the world* for the Messiah's advent. All those high and mighty folks listed in verse 1 were involved whether they knew it or not. They were going to come under the aegis of God's Christ, whether they knew it or not, whether they liked it or not.

On this Advent Sunday, here is a message that is bracing for us to consider. Because today, too, there is resistance to the idea that the gospel has global implications. "Christmas" has become a widespread phenomenon, of course, but mostly just in the sense of promoting a generic spirit of goodness, generosity, good cheer. You can even celebrate Christmas without reference to the gospel, without singing or talking about Jesus. People do this all the time. I mean, the Griswold family doesn't seem terribly pious, do they? If you want Christmas to be also about the birth of some alleged Savior in a barn two thousand years ago—I mean, if that kind of story turns your crank—well and good, but leave the rest of us out of it, thank you very much.

Across the spectrum of society, therefore, it's acceptable if we Christians want to zero in on Jesus over the holidays, but we need to restrict the scope of our message. If it works for us, that's fine, but don't pretend that it has anything to do with anyone else. If we stay in our little corner, we can say, sing, and believe pretty much anything we want. But the moment we stray, the second we suggest that Jesus is the Lord of every person everywhere, the world turns on us.

So long as John the Baptist restricted himself to teaching folks out in the middle of nowhere, he was safe. But John knew that his message of repentance had to apply to everybody or else it applied to nobody. If the Christ whose way John was preparing could not speak to Herod's situation, then neither could the Christ speak to any situation.

The church has also long insisted that John the Baptist is an absolutely necessary character in the Advent drama. But so often even we in the church forget this. Even most Christians are not completely sure they want John at Christmas. And so we don't generally put John on any Christmas cards. We have no John the Baptist Christmas tree ornaments. No child plays John in Christmas programs, and he's nowhere to be seen on front yard manger displays (though Frosty and Santa have been known to put in a manger-side appearance). John is too untidy, too dangerous for Christmas. Invite John to your holiday party and he'll spill eggnog all over your Persian rug as he flails his arms around talking about the need to repent.

And yet by grace, God does bring us before John. And by grace, we are able to hear his message and actually be comforted by the message that our lives—not just parts of them but the totality of our lives—really are engulfed by the goodness of God in Christ. And this is profoundly good news, isn't it?

After all, perhaps it has forever been true but in recent times Advent and ultimately Christmas get celebrated beneath very cloudy skies, and I'm not talking about West Michigan meteorology. Terrorist attacks abound as do mass shootings about every other week. Ugly partisan political fighting goes on and on. In so many ways this world does not look like it has already been visited by God's Christ, by the Messiah. Ours is so very often a tear-drenched Advent, a fearful Advent, an uncertain Advent. We wait in hope that Christ will advent onto this world a second time, because that hope alone validates our doing anything to celebrate his first coming. I mean, if he's not coming again, who cares he came the first time, right?

And as we do this waiting, as we cling to this hope, can we be assured that God still has the whole world—and the entirety of our lives—in his hands? John the

Baptist storms onto our Advent stage today to tell us "Yes!" The reason John was so direct, so uncompromising, so fierce is because he knew that the Messiah whose way he was preparing was God's ultimate answer to everything.

Because of all the tragedy and terror of the wider world, because of ISIS, because of shootings at social service centers, because we cannot go to work or step onto an airplane and know for sure we're safe—because of all that, Advent is definitely a test to see what it is we believe. What do we know to be true in Christ? Do we really believe that the child born of Mary is who he says he is, is already now ruling the galaxies as Lord and King, and is coming back to make all things new? Is God giving us enough grace to believe that? I believe he does give us that grace, and for all his off-putting, fire-snorting ways, John the Baptist helps us embrace just such a wild and wonderful faith.

We celebrate this Advent that Jesus came to redeem us. He came to save us and to save not just bits and pieces of our lives but the whole of them. Jesus came to address not just some of our worst nightmares but all of them. He came to sacrifice himself, not to give us a little hope here and there but eternal hope. What's the line from that one Christmas carol we sing: "the hopes and fears of all the years are met in thee tonight"? Yes, that's right. All the hopes, all the fears. All of it.

And John helps us see this anew today by bringing us face to face with sin, with reality, and with the Christ of God who alone can take it all on. We want John. We need John this Advent. To riff on Fred Craddock, John is the one in the Advent and Christmas drama who forces the moment of truth on us. John brings us into direct contact with the living God, which is what everyone wants and what no one wants. When John barges into your life, he changes everything. John brings us the clarity of grace.

To make that point, Craddock once told the story of a missionary family in China who was forced to leave the country sometime after the communists took over. One day a band of soldiers knocked on the door and told this missionary, his wife, and his children that they had two hours to pack up before these troops would escort them to the train station. They would be permitted to take with them only two hundred pounds of stuff.

Thus began two hours of family wrangling and bickering—what should they take? What about this vase? It's a family heirloom, so we've got to take the vase. Well, maybe so, but this typewriter is brand new and we're not about to leave that behind. What about some books? Got to take a few of them along. On and on it went, putting stuff on the bathroom scale and taking it off until finally they had a pile of possessions that totaled two hundred pounds on the dot.

At the appointed hour the soldiers returned. "Are you ready?" they asked. "Yes." "Did you weigh your stuff?" "Yes, we did." "Two hundred pounds?" "Yes, two hundred pounds on the dot." "Did you weigh the kids?" "Um...no." "Weigh the kids!"

And in an instant the vase, the typewriter, and the books all became trash. *Trash!* None of it meant anything compared to the surpassing value of the children. Sometimes we all face "the moment of truth." Sometimes events crash into our lives in so shocking a way that we are instantly forced to view all of life in a new light. Suddenly what had previously been of value comes to mean absolutely nothing—indeed, we're only too happy to leave it behind.[6]

That was the effect John the Baptist had on all who listened to him. And yet something within us says, "Goodness, aren't the holidays stressful enough without having to deal with this too? It's hard enough to steel ourselves to be around Aunt Bessie again all day on Christmas! Do we really have to let John in the door too!?"

John is too shrill. If we let John in the door, he'll wake the baby in the manger. Then again, if we do *not* let John in, if we will not or cannot tolerate his uncompromising message that Christ is Lord of all, then that baby in the manger may as well just go on sleeping forever and ever. Because if we can't let John in, we're not ready for the baby to wake up anyway. If we don't like what John says, we won't like what that baby will eventually say either. And then, *then*, Christmas is over before it really began. Amen.

December 16, 2018–Third Sunday of Advent

Zephaniah 3:14-20; Isaiah 12:2-6; Philippians 4:4-7; Luke 3:7-18

Call to Worship (from Zephaniah 3 and Isaiah 12)

The Lord, the king of Israel, is in your midst;

Do not be afraid.

God is indeed my salvation;

I will trust and won't be afraid.

The Lord has removed your judgment;

He has turned away your enemy,

He is a warrior bringing victory.

The Lord is my strength and my shield;

He has become my salvation.

I will thank the Lord and call on his name!

The Lord your God is in your midst,

He will calm you with his love;

He will rejoice over you with singing.

We shout and sing for joy,

Because the holy one of Israel is among us.

We will trust him and will not be afraid!

Prayer for Illumination

Ever present God:

As we open your word,

Open our eyes so that we might see both ourselves

and the truth of your life-changing promises more clearly.

And if, for some reason, your word does not seem to apply to us today,

Give us the special gift of your Spirit

So that we might store it up in our hearts

For when we need it the most.

In the name of Jesus and by the power of the Holy Spirit we pray,

Amen.

Preaching Theme

The Apostle Paul tells us not to be anxious—not to worry—about anything. But we tend to be people who worry about everything. We worry about what will happen if someone doesn't show up for the big Christmas dinner (and also about what might happen if they do!). We worry about getting into the right school and about the financial aid package coming through. We worry about the cancer coming back and about our company being bought out. We worry about the security of our jobs and the safety of our kids. With so much to worry about, how is it that Paul can tell us not to worry and not to be anxious?

When Dietrich Bonhoeffer sat in his Nazi prison cell, he penned a poem that included these words to the effect that we fearlessly wait, come what may, because God is with us on every new day. Paul, writing to the church in Philippi from his own prison cell, says something similar. Why is it that we need not be anxious or afraid? Is it because whatever we are worried about is really "no big deal"? Or because God guarantees that everything will turn out for the best? Or even because God won't give us any more hardship or pain than we can handle? No. Paul says that we need not be anxious or afraid because "the Lord is near." That is the good news to which everything else in this text is tethered. "The Lord is near," even while we wait for him to come in all his fullness. In fact, Paul says, he is as close as a prayer. And when God's children take their worries and anxieties to the Lord in prayer, he will exchange their anxiety for his peace and calm their worried hearts with his love (Zeph 3:17).

Secondary Preaching Themes

The sight of a mother cradling a squirming child in her arms and singing lullabies over him until he finally goes limp may be one of the sweetest and most serene things we can witness in this life. It's a scene as old as time, and perhaps it is what the prophet Zephaniah had in mind when he wrote one of the final (and most famous!) verses of his book: "The LORD your God is in your midst....He will create calm with his love; he will rejoice over you with singing" (Zeph 3:17). When heard in the context of the other lectionary passages for the Third Sunday of Advent, God's often anxious and worried children can receive these words as an invitation to climb into the lap of their heavenly Father so that he might sooth them with the songs of his love and care. Then, having heard these songs, they might offer him one of their own, perhaps borrowing words from the prophet Isaiah: "God is indeed my salvation; I will trust and won't be afraid" (Isa 12:2).

While the Apostle Paul seems to be doing everything he can to free us from anxiety, John the Baptist seems to be doing everything he can to create anxiety in us. John's words are so full of alarm, he seems so determined to set us on edge. For John, the news that "the Lord is near" is not only a promise that ought to comfort the afflicted. It is also a promise that ought to afflict the comfortable!

Parting Blessing

Do not be anxious about anything;

For the Lord is near.

Do not be afraid,

For the Lord is near.

The Lord your God will quiet you with his love;

He will rejoice over you with singing.

He will be your strength and salvation.

Do not be afraid.

But trust that the blessing of almighty God—Father, Son, and Holy Spirit—

Will be with you always.

Amen.

December 23, 2018–Fourth Sunday of Advent

Passages: Micah 5:2-5a; Luke 1:46b-55 or Psalm 80:1-7; Hebrews 10:5-10; Luke 1:39-45 (46-55)

Gathering Prayer (adaption of Luke 1:46b-55)

With all my heart I glorify the Lord!

In the depths of who I am I rejoice in God my Savior.

God has looked with favor on the low status of his servant.

Holy is the Lord

God shows mercy to everyone,

from one generation to the next.

God has shown strength…

Scattering those with arrogant thoughts and proud inclinations.

And pulling the powerful down from their thrones to lift up the lowly.

God fills those who are hungry with good things

and sends the greedy away empty-handed.

God has swiftly come to the aid of humanity,

Showing us mercy time and time again.

Amen.

Preaching Theme

A common experience, a shared expectancy, is presented in the narrative of Mary's visitation with Elizabeth. Two mothers different in age, attached by blood, yet uniquely challenged by societal milieu are connected by their unrealized promised potential of their sons. Their meeting is the result of divine impartation and for purposes of affirmation. A redeeming of personhood and significance experienced by one considered less because of age and barrenness. The second, bothered and vulnerable to the unethical, yet permitted, cultural practices of devaluing of women, particularly the unattached.

The account records that Elizabeth's child, later known as John, leaps for joy while in utero—a reverent response to being in the presence of the "sent one" for whom he serves as forerunner. The power of the Spirit is highlighted and transcends, marking a revival of prophetic activity. Such activity has been seemingly absent from the lived reality of persons during this period. This text captures the essence of the Advent season: the promise of something and someone that will not simply make life better—rather, the assurance of the Word incarnate and of a life full of meaning, a promise of life lived and of life everlasting. Elizabeth's prophetic encouragement and her respect for Mary's sacred identity, "mother of my Lord," and her recognition that Mary is "blessed" echoes across generations reminding us that those not named are also blessed.

Secondary Preaching Themes

In Micah 5:2-5a, we are reminded that even in times of despair, God has a plan to deliver us. With the nation's capital under attack, God reassures the people of Israel that everything is going to be alright because help is on the way. Ironically, that help is going to come from a place that is home to "the least significant of Judah's forces" (v. 2). Bethlehem, which held little significance outside of being the birthplace of King David, would now give birth to a new king. One who will bring restoration and be known throughout the earth as the Prince of Peace.

When we have wronged another person, we often find ourselves reflecting on ways to make amends. Usually, a simple apology or act of repentance will suffice, but sometimes those displays cannot easily reverse the damage that was done. In Hebrews 10:5-10, Paul helps us understand that although there was a time when our acts of repentance may not have carried much weight in the eyes of God, Jesus's ultimate sacrifice has restored us into right relationship with God for good.

Benediction

O God who created us for thyself,

May we be found where you

Bless us as you lead, lift, and love us

By means of your grace and mercy

In the name of the God of all,

Amen.

December 25, 2018–
Nativity of the Lord/
Christmas Day

Passages: Isaiah 9:2-7; Psalm 96; Titus 2:11-14; Luke 2:1-14 (15-20)

Gathering Prayer

Almighty God, as we gather together in worship

Help us to be reminded of your humility

So that we might also be humble.

Help us to be reminded of your light

So that we might also be light.

Help us be reminded of your love

So that we might love one another.

Amen.

Preaching Theme

In the face of oppressive systems, God reigns sovereign through acts of fulfillment of prophecy as foretold in first testament texts in Isaiah 7 and Micah 5. Amid the world's crisis, Christ appears by uncharacteristic means—virgin teenage mother—and in the nontouristy, nonglamorous place of Bethlehem. He is born into poverty—not of a mere economic nature, but also of political disenfranchisement, societal chaos, and cultural-religious peril. The birth of Christ in a child of color serves notice to the world that a change is taking place. Luke intentionally connects the divinely inspired birth with Caesar Augustus's decree, making it a world event of eternal consequence. Jesus marks more than a threat to the empire, as evidenced by the subsequent instituting of marshal law, targeted deportation, and genocide against male children of color. However, with respect to contemporary themes, Caesar's tax decree serves as the principal reason for Joseph and Mary's travels to Bethlehem. In other words, economic and geopolitical hardships coupled with unreconciled religious beliefs and individual practices bring into question both the emotional, marital, and citizen status of this couple. Jesus's modest entry into a manic world made a major difference. His humble beginning will eventually give way to a heartfelt ethical life committed to others, an inhumane death, and ultimately, heavenly reign. But for now in the text, he who is our protection is protected. The one who clothes us is swaddled in strips of cloth. He who is to carry the weight of our sins is sinless and coddled…in a space left for animals.

Secondary Preaching Themes

There is nothing more frustrating than getting up in the middle of the night to use the bathroom or grab a midnight snack and stubbing your toe on the corner of the bed. Most of the time, this happens because despite how well we think we know the layout of that room, we still need light to help us get around it safely. That said, most of us were walking around life in darkness before we met Jesus. And yet, despite answering God's call to be in covenant relationship, we as individuals and members of the larger body of Christ are still finding our way around in the dark. Isaiah 9:2-7 reminds us that on this day a child was given unto us and that child is the light of the world!

As we remember the arrival of the infant Jesus, let us not forget that the child did not arrive empty handed. The grace of God arrived in an overflow room reserved for livestock and brought with him the salvation of humankind. Paul reminds us that the example set forth by this child, "educates us so that we can live sensible, ethical, and godly lives right now by rejecting ungodly lives and the desires of this world" (v. 12). In taking full advantage of Jesus's teachings, we can become a living testimony of God's grace (Titus 2:11-14).

Benediction

Anointed One whom we seek and who also seeks us;

Our progenitor, grantor of life, light, and love;

You who are our promised protection, provision, and peace;

Bless each of us now and forever forward,

Amen.

December 30, 2018

Passages: *1 Samuel 2:18-20, 26; Psalm 148; Colossians 3:12-17; Luke 2:41-52*

Gathering Prayer

Most Holy God, we run to be in your presence greeted by your love.

We rejoice in the joy of you.

Affirm in us your purposes. Reveal to us your plans.

Assure us of your promise that forever will fill our days with thee.

Amen.

Preaching Theme

Luke presents a maturing Jesus. Here Jesus's humanity and divinity are spotlighted. Luke describes this existential tension as a "mystery." This mystery is not simply visited upon the biblical character of Jesus; rather it is the inherent nature of relationship between humanity and God. Jesus's humanity and deity are highlighted on the occasion of his bar mitzvah—acknowledging being "a son of the law." Jesus seemed aware, even if his parents were not, of both his relationship and sense of calling with God.

Honoring tradition, Jesus and his family, in accordance with commandments, travel to Jerusalem to celebrate Passover. In faithfulness to practice, Mary and Joseph, along with a caravan of believers, endure the audacious journey from Nazareth to Jerusalem. At the conclusion of the seven-day festival, Mary and Joseph set out for home unknowingly without their newly minted teen. Once they realized Jesus's absence, they returned to Jerusalem and searched for the boy for three days. On the third day Jesus is discovered in temple sharing in discourse and intellectual query with the elder teachers. Jesus's presence and presentations among this scholarly circle had everyone "standing out of themselves." His divine genius and giftedness is validated by all in attendance. His parents, on the other hand, are somewhat unimpressed, as expressed by Mary's reprimanding Jesus for not staying "in a child's place." To which Jesus replies that his rightful place is "in my Father's house." It is in the temple of God that he and all who serve God should find themselves. More importantly, it is Jesus's understanding of mission or strong sense of duty that made him seek validation or approval of the ultimate progenitor over earthly covering.

Secondary Preaching Themes

As children of God made in the image of the Most High, we are called to live in a way that is reflective of the new life we have in Christ. In Colossians 3, the Apostle Paul highlights five virtues: compassion, kindness, humility, gentleness, and patience. Paul goes on to state that love is the bond of unity. In our contemporary context and language, we recognize these virtues are the components of empathy—it is our openness to seeing and learning from those around us. It is our ability to put our ego and those things that make us feel uncomfortable or impatient to the side so that we can truly hear the other. When we approach one another in love, we open ourselves to connection and to a righteous relationship, which pushes us toward justice. In our dealings with one another, in the church and outside of the church, all of these virtues should shine through in our willingness to limit ourselves in favor of right and righteous relationship in our community.

There is something significant about a parent's willingness allowing/encouraging their child to serve in the house of God. Instead of accidentally leaving their child behind like Mary and Joseph, Hannah and Elkanah entrusted their child to Eli as a sacrifice to the Lord. Hannah's child served as a sacrifice for answered prayer. Mary's child would serve as a sacrifice for all humankind. Both young men grew in the favor of Lord and both women's sacrifices were met with blessings from on high (1 Sam 2:18-20, 26).

Benediction/Responsive Prayer ("Archbishop Oscar Romero Prayer: A Step Along the Way" by Bishop Ken Untener of Saginaw)[7]

It helps, now and then, to step back and take a long view. The kingdom is not only beyond our efforts, it is even beyond our vision.

We accomplish in our lifetime only a tiny fraction of the magnificent enterprise that is God's work. Nothing we do is complete, which is a way of saying that the kingdom always lies beyond us.

No statement says all that could be said.

No prayer fully expresses our faith.

No program accomplishes the church's mission.

No set of goals and objectives includes everything.

This is what we are about.

We plant the seeds that one day will grow.

We water seeds already planted, knowing that they hold future promise.

We lay foundations that will need further development.

We provide yeast that produces far beyond our capabilities.

We cannot do everything, and there is a sense of liberation in realizing that.

This enables us to do something, and to do it very well.

It may be incomplete, but it is a beginning, a step along the way, an opportunity for the Lord's grace to enter and do the rest.

We may never see the end results, but that is the difference between the master builder and the worker.

We are workers, not master builders; ministers, not messiahs.

We are prophets of a future not our own.

Excerpt from *SHE: Five Keys to Unlock the Power of Women in Ministry* by Karoline M. Lewis

In this book Karoline Lewis seeks to explore some of the particular issues that women in ministry face in an effort to help women, and everyone in the church, accept and under-stand the unique gifts and perspectives women bring to preaching, exegesis, and ministry generally. The book is organized around five "keys," and this excerpt comes from the first such key, which Lewis describes as "The Truth About Women, the Bible, Feminism, and Theology."

....

Any interpretation of the Bible inevitably has to begin with the individual. Self-interpretation is absolutely crucial for biblical interpretation. Yet, this is a difficult place to start for most. It takes hard and honest work. Most of us do not want to admit how ideological we are. Truthfully, most of us do not want to admit we even have ideologies. We assume that ideologies are inherently bad, that to be ideological or to be named an ideologue presumes an uncompromising and dogmatic stance in the world. This can certainly be true. Yet, what is also true is that we all are ideologues in some way. We all have working ideologies, or philosophies and principles, if you will. The truth-telling that needs to happen in the church and in ministry is owning up to them. Biblical interpretation, especially interpretive claims that justify certain actions, systems, and practices in the church, inevitably end up going horribly askew when ideologies go unchecked or, worse, treated as though they do not exist. Somehow, and still, too many who claim the authority to interpret the Bible insist they do not bring any influences into that interpretation; that with the Bible, one is able to bracket out any bias so as to be able to read the Bible objectively.

An illustration of this truth may be helpful at this point. There is a museum in Los Angeles called the museum of tolerance. After purchasing your ticket for admission into the museum you descend an escalator to get to the museum's entrance. At the entrance is a docent standing between two double doors. Over one set of double doors is the sign "prejudiced." Over the other set of double doors is the sign "not prejudiced." The docent then invites you to choose through which double doors you would like to enter the museum. As it turns out, the "not prejudiced" doors are locked because we all hold prejudices. This is the first truth you learn in this museum experience. We are prejudiced and it is a falsehood to tell ourselves that we are not. This is also true for our ideological selves, which live and function in the systems and institutions we set in place to organize ourselves, ideologies included...especially the church.

Practically, the first task in assessing who you are as a biblical interpreter is to begin to list all of those things that shape who you are. These include, but are not exhausted by, the following: gender, race, education, denomination, tradition, sexual orientation, demographics, health, and family. All of these factors influence who we are and therefore what we bring to any interaction with the Bible. The question becomes which of these factors are more operative than others in how you interpret your world.

Your gender shapes the way you read. Regardless of our quests for universality and equality among the Bible's readers, the truth is women will resonate with different aspects of the Bible than men. The other truth is that there have not been enough women publicly interpreting the Bible to bring these resonances into any kind of balance with what is typically and traditionally heard in (male) interpretations.

As a woman interpreting the Bible in the public context of ministry, you have an obligation to give voice to interpretations that have either not been allowed or uttered aloud. This does not mean that every Bible study or every sermon needs to be about women, have a story about women, or present feminine imagery for God. in fact, if this becomes the expectation about how you engage the Bible, it can quickly be assumed that interpretations that prioritize women and women's issues are the only ways in which you can talk about the Bible. At best, you are the one who talks about "women's issues." At worst, your influence devolves into an aspect of tokenism. This has to be a shared task by you and by your colleagues in ministry, regardless of gender. At the same time, if you do not tend these other voices in scripture and acknowledge publicly that there are other interpreters besides men who care what scripture has to say, there is a good chance that no one will. If you do not lift up stories about women in the Bible, preach the texts that have women characters, and look for ways to imagine God's femininity, evidence shows that little to no attention will be given to women in the Bible or feminine imagery for God. A woman in ministry has a responsibility, in part, for this tending. We would like it to be different. We would like it to be a given that we should not have to shoulder this responsibility alone. The truth is, we are not there yet, and if you do not do this work, who will?

Practically, what does this mean as an interpreter of the Bible? Some of what is presented here will be outlined further in the discussion of the role of feminism for women in ministry. At this point, for the sake of the individual context as a biblical interpreter, it means listening deeply for the voices that call from the margins. It means giving voice to those who have been silenced or who never had a voice while still recognizing what it's like to have someone who's never had your experience speak for you. It means trusting in yourself that your interpretations can make a difference. It means trusting that your voice, your voice *as a woman*, matters, and that how you fill in gaps and where you locate yourself in the biblical texts matters deeply for many, especially for the many who have only heard one voice and have never trusted their own. Our interpretations of the Bible do shape the way we live our lives and many in our pews have not heard that their lives matter when it comes to the Bible.

Excerpt from *Preaching and the Human Condition: Loving God, Self, and Others* by O. Wesley Allen, Jr.

In this book O. Wesley Allen, Jr. considers how to preach to the human condition in terms of the vertical, horizontal, and inner horizons of our lives. In this excerpt Allen begins to discuss the vertical dimension of the human condition in terms of our human relationship with God and the ways that relationship has consistently gone awry due to human sinfulness.

....

We fail to trust, indeed are unable to trust, in God even though we are utterly dependent upon God. The result, then, is that we place our trust elsewhere. We have a wide range of sinful actions against God, but structurally speaking, all acts of disobedience and rebellion are really expressions of idolatry. The Decalogue opens with four commandments that all deal with this fact. The Israelites were commanded to have no other gods before Adonai, make and worship no idols, make no wrongful use of Adonai's name, and observe the Sabbath (Ex 20:1-11). To break any of these commandments is to place something else before God. The fact of the matter is, however, that no matter how well intentioned we are when we say, "As for me and my household, we will serve the Lord" (Josh 24:15), we fail over and over again and are unable to succeed in our willingness and ability to trust in God and God's will for us. We, knowingly and unknowingly, serve and worship something else as a means of self-service and self-worship. The sovereign God cannot not be molded into Santa Claus or a good-luck charm. Thus we turn, over and over again, to golden calves, patriotism, family ties, money, privilege, position, and the likes because these gods can be made to serve us. As Paul says, "The desire to do good is inside of me, but I can't do it. I don't do the good that I want to do, but I do the evil that I don't want to do" (Rom 7:18b-19).

Our failure in our vertical relationship with God, however, is not the last word on this dimension of the human condition. Our sinful nature is answered by God's character. Our worship of lesser gods (including ourselves) is countered by the one, true God. Because God is just and righteous in God's will for humanity, God judges our iniquity. But God does not forget our utter dependence on God even when we do. God remains *pro nobis* even when we turn against God. God remembers God's covenants with us. God brings us to repentance. God forgives our sin. And God reconciles us to God's self. *This* is the last word on the vertical dimension of the human condition. But such good news can only be proclaimed, heard, and experienced if word of our sinfulness is named first.

Biblical

Throughout Israel's history as told and interpreted by the various writers in the Hebrew Bible, human sinfulness is portrayed in Technicolor fashion. Adam and Eve disobey God's direct order. The people try to build a tower to the heavens to make a name for themselves. After God rescues the slaves from Egypt, they fashion a golden calf in the wilderness. Over and over again, the Israelites turn to foreign gods such as Ba'al. Individuals, tribes, priests, and kings are all indicted.

Yet God's *hesed* (steadfast loving-kindness) is continually extended to the people even though they turn away from God. We turn from God, and God establishes covenants with the people through Noah, Abraham and Sarah, Moses, and David, and reestablishes and reaffirms this covenantal relationship through the prophets. Even when our disobedience pushes God to announce, "You are not my people, and I am not your God" (Hos 1:9), God does so in order that God can restore the relationship and reclaim us as God's people ("In the place where it was said to them, 'You are not my people,' it will be said to them, 'Children of the living God'" [Hos 1:10]). God judges so that God might forgive. And forgive God does, over and over again, reconciling the idolatrous and self-serving to Godself.

The New Testament likewise portrays our sinfulness and God's rescue in relation to the vertical dimension. The Christ event can be interpreted through the lens of the vertical dimension of the human condition as an expression of God's reconciliation of us to Godself. Substitutionary and satisfaction views of the atonement that grow out of New Testament metaphors are attempts to name that humanity has broken our relationship with God through idolatrous disobedience and rebellion and are an offense to God's righteousness...yet, God's will to be reconciled to us is greater than our condition of sinfulness. Through Christ's birth, ministry, crucifixion (especially the crucifixion!), and resurrection, God atones us—makes us "at one" with God. Through the faithfulness of the one who ate with tax collectors and sinners, we are justified while we are yet guilty. Even though we are unable to be in right relationship with God, God proclaims through the Christ event that God is in right relationship with us. Salvation experienced in terms of being put in right relation with God thus results in well-being in terms both of this earthly existence and eternal life.

Homiletical

It is a difficult task for preachers to convince their congregations that they are idolaters. Oh, it is easy to find examples of our idolatry to use in sermons. It is simply hard for us to recognize or admit that such examples are really idolatrous.

I continue to find Paul Tillich's classic description of idolatry useful for helping people today intellectually grasp that people (maybe not themselves) are idolatrous as surely as if they sacrificed their best calf at an altar stationed before a bronze statue.[1] Tillich argues that all humans have a hierarchy of concerns. We value our car more than our bicycle, our home more than our car, and our family more than our home. Not only is there nothing wrong with such a hierarchy, it is a perfectly normal and healthy way of shaping our priorities. Yet something must be (and always is) at the top of the hierarchy. There is something that I hold more valuable than everything else. There is something that concerns me more than anything else concerns me. Understood in this way, Tillich can say that there is no such thing as an atheist, because everyone has an ultimate concern, everyone has a god she or he worships and serves. Conversely, it could be argued that there is no such thing as a person who is not an idolater, because we all place other concerns above our concern for God, at least from time to time.

While Tillich's description of ultimate concern (when used repeatedly in the pulpit) can help a congregation understand idolatry in the abstract, we must admit that there is a difference between understanding the issue in our heads and recognizing it in our hearts when it is staring us back in the mirror. We can understand the "dynamic" of idolatry, see it practiced by others, and yet be oblivious to our own captivity by it. We humans have an amazing ability to deny the very conditions that damage our well-being.

Excerpt from *Introduction to the Practice of African American Preaching* by Frank Thomas

Frank Thomas has a passion to share with the world the unique genius and ethos of the African American preaching tradition. In this book Thomas traces the history of this style of preaching first by giving readers what he calls a "bus tour" of the tradition as it moved from an oral to an oral-written style. The rest of the book explores the early influences on African American preaching and how it developed a rhetorical and theological manner of gospel communication that was highly participatory in proclaiming a message of hope and victory that was celebrated with great joy in every sermon. In this excerpt Thomas lays out what he regards as the six most central characteristics of this preaching tradition.

....

In the introduction, I mentioned that as part of my research for this book, I convened separately twenty-two homileticians, who teach and publish scholarship on African American preaching, and twenty-five African American pastors, who practice preaching to congregations on a weekly basis. I followed a similar format in both discussions and asked each group to respond to the same three important and critical questions concerning African American preaching. Of the three questions, the one that is relevant for this chapter is: What is black preaching?

In regards to both groups, we did not settle the question of defining exactly what black preaching is. As a matter of fact, we concluded that we were not sure that the question would ever be definitively settled once and for all. We resolved that each generation of pastors and scholars must wrestle with the question and make a contribution to the definition of this elusive and yet potent tradition. We acknowledged that the African American preaching tradition has been shaped by faithful responses to centuries of racial, sexual, social, cultural, political, economic, and gender oppression, and as a result, is uniquely able to minister to all people, and especially hurting and oppressed people in America, and all over the globe. But, for the most part, a definition was hard to pin down. In this chapter, I would like to offer my contribution to the discussion through the application of critical methods from the field of rhetoric, namely rhetorical criticism, to an actual preached sermon...

When we consider characteristics of the African American preaching tradition, I would argue that there are at least six: the centrality of the Bible, the importance of experiential preaching, existential exegesis, inspiration of the Holy Spirit, suspense that leads to celebration, and the performative nature of the sermon.[1] Again, because these characteristics have been generally discussed in other works, I will only mention them briefly:

1. The centrality of the Bible—this is not to be mistaken for a rigid biblical literalism. The Bible is seen as *the* inspired and dynamic source for understanding the world and *the* wise guide for life's decisions. Cleophus J. LaRue suggests: "More than a mere sources for texts, in black preaching, the Bible is the single most important source of language, imagery, and story for the sermon."[2]

2. The importance of experiential preaching—the Bible comes alive by means of an eyewitness style of picture painting and narration. The preacher stirs the five senses, and as a result, the hearer does not just hear about John the Baptist in past biblical times, John the Baptist is present in the room, seen, heard, touched, and felt by all. I heard James Forbes Jr. tell the story that Gardner C. Taylor was preaching the biblical story of the prodigal son. In a particularly poignant moment, Forbes recounts that Taylor said, "Look, the boy is coming up the road now!" Forbes says he turned around, looked to the back of the church, and saw the boy coming up the road. The African American sermon is experiential.

3. Existential exegesis—a particular form of exegesis that joins biblical scholarship to existential human need. African American preaching operates from the perspective of a close observation of the Bible and human need, which directs the sermon to resolve existential concern by exegesis of the text. The sermon is never academic alone, but exegesis addresses human need and illustrates for hearers the true meaning of life and living.

4. The inspiration of the Holy Spirit—the preacher is dependent on a power beyond the preacher's power. The Holy Spirit ultimately shapes and delivers the message through the preacher. The sermon is not simply the words of a human being, but the very voice of God speaks through the preacher.

5. Suspense that leads to celebration—the preacher structures the sermon to hold suspense as long as possible, and after the suspense is resolved, the preacher celebrates the good news with a powerful and uplifting conclusion. The weight that the black church places on a powerful conclusion to a message is unparalleled in any culture. The majority of the time the close is reserved for pure celebration and close the preacher must.

6. The performative nature of the sermon—the word of God must be "embodied" in the total person of the preacher, including head (rationality), heart (emotionality), and body (physicality). The word must be incarnated in the total person of the preacher and not just the rational aspects of the preacher's being, hence the sermon, in the best sense of the word, is performed.

Notes

February

1. Rowan Williams, *Being Christian: Baptism, Bible, Eucharist, and Prayer* (Grand Rapids: Eerdmans, 2014), 11.

March

1. Mayra Rivera, "Glory: The First Passion of Theology?" in *Polydoxy: Theology of Multiplicity and Relation*, ed. Catherine Keller and Laurel C. Schneider (London and New York: Routledge, 2011), 168.

2. Saint Augustine, *Confessions*, trans. Henry Chadwick (Oxford: Oxford University Press, 1992), X.vi.8, 183. Emphasis added.

3. Howard Thurman, *The Inward Journey* (Richmond, IN: Friends United Press, 1961), 113.

4. John Wesley, "Salvation by Faith," www.umcmission.org/Find-Resources /John-Wesley-Sermons/Sermon-1-Salvation-by-Faith.

5. Dennis T. Olson, *Interpretation: Numbers* (Louisville: Westminster John Knox, 1996), 136.

6. Alan C. Mitchell, *Sacra Pagina: Hebrews* (Collegeville, MN: Liturgical Press, 2007), 141–44.

7. Kathleen M. O'Connor, "Jeremiah" in *The New Interpreter's Study Bible* (Nashville: Abingdon, 2003), 104.

8. Alex Varughese and Mitchel Modine, *Jeremiah 26–52: A Commentary in the Wesleyan Tradition* (Kansas City, MO: Beacon Hill, 2010), 151.

9. William L. Holladay, *Hermeneia:* Jeremiah 2 (Minneapolis, MN: Fortress, 1989), 198.

April

1. Anne Lamott, H*elp, Thanks, Wow: The Three Essential Prayers* (New York: Riverhead, 2012).

2. John Donne: "A Valediction: of Weeping." Poetry Foundation, 15 Jan 2017, https://www.poetryfoundation.org/resources/learning/core-poems/detail/44132.

3. Anne Lamott, *Plan B: Further Thoughts on Faith* (New York: Riverhead, 2006).

4. Franz H. Messerli, "Chocolate Consumption, Cognitive Function, and Nobel Laureates," *New England Journal of Medicine* 367, no. 16 (October 18, 2012): 1562–1564.

5. Craig Barnes, "Savior at Large (John 20:1-18)," *The Christian Century*, March 13-20, 2002, p. 16.

May

1. From the Samaritan's Purse video "Rescuers Lift Refugees to Safety," http://video.samaritanspurse.org/rescuers-lift-refugees-to-safety/.

July

1. Marcus J. Borg and John Dominic Crossan, *The First Paul: Reclaiming the Radical Visionary behind the Church's Conservative Icon* (San Francisco: Harper-Collins, 2009).

September

1. Eugene Peterson, *The Message: The New Testament in Contemporary English* (Colorado Springs: Navpress, 1993), 480.

2. Nelson Mandela, *Long Walk to Freedom* (New York: Little, Brown & Co., 2008 ebook edition), 22.

3. C. S. Lewis, *Reflections on the Psalms* (New York: Harcourt, Brace, and World Inc., 1958), 63.

November

1. https://www.crcna.org/sites/default/files/our_world_belongs_to_god_2008_version.pdf.

December

1. Cornelius Plantinga Jr., "Between Two Advents: In the Interim (Luke 21:28)," www.religion-online.org/showarticle.asp?title=2020, accessed July 29, 2016.

2. Paraphrased from *Grace (Eventually)* (New York: Riverhead, 2007), 56. Actual quotation reads, "My pastor, Veronica, says that believing isn't the hard part; waiting on God is."

3. Originally in Lewis B. Smedes, *Standing on the Promises* (Nashville: Thomas Nelson, 1998), quoted in Plantinga, "Between Two Advents."

4. Barbara Brown Taylor, *Speaking of Sin* (Boston: Cowley Publications, 2000), 66.

5. http://nationalpres.org/sites/default/files/sermon_bulletins/1997.12.21 .Barnes_0.pdf, accessed August 6, 2016. Emphasis added.

6. Fred B. Craddock, "Have You Ever Heard John Preach?" in *A Chorus of Witnesses: Model Sermons for Today's Preacher,* Thomas G. Long and Cornelius Plantinga, Jr., editors (Grand Rapids: Eerdmans, 1994), 41.

7. www.usccb.org/prayer-and-worship/prayers-and-devotions/prayers/arch bishop_romero_prayer.cfm.

Excerpt from *Preaching and the Human Condition*

1. Paul Tillich, *The Dynamics of Faith* (New York: Harper, 1957).

Excerpt from *Introduction to the Practice of African American Preaching*

1. Five of these characteristics are listed in *Preaching with Sacred Fire: The Anthology of African American Preaching 1750–Present* (New York: W. W. Norton and Company, 2010), 7–8, and the sixth characteristic was added in the latest edition of *They Like to Never Quit Praisin' God: The Role of Celebration in Preaching* (Cleveland: United Church Press, 2013), 1–4.

2. Cleophus LaRue, *The Heart of Black Preaching* (Louisville: Westminister John Knox, 1999), 10.

Contributors: Lectionary Sermon and Worship Helps

Shelia Bouie-Sledge—Associate Pastor, Salem United Methodist Church, Saint Louis, MO
August 5, 2018

Josh Davis—Multiethnic Worship Leader, Founder, Proskuneo, Clarkston, GA
April 15, 2018; April 22, 2018; April 29, 2018; May 6, 2018

Yvette Davis—Pastor, Grace United Methodist Church, Harrisburg, PA
June 10, 2018; June 17, 2018; June 24, 2018; July 1, 2018

Magrey deVega—Pastor, Hyde Park United Methodist Church, Tampa, FL
July 8, 2018; July 15, 2018; July 22, 2018; July 29, 2018

Chelsey Harmon—Pastor, Christ Community Church, Nanaimo, BC, Canada
May 10, 2018; May 13, 2018; May 20, 2018; May 27, 2018

Scott Hoezee, General Editor—Director, The Center for Excellence in Preaching, Calvin
Theological Seminary, Grand Rapids, MI
February 18, 2018; June 3, 2018; August 12, 2018; August 19, 2018; August 26, 2018

Juan Huertas—Pastor, Grace Community United Methodist Church, Shreveport, LA
March 29, 2018; March 30, 2018; April 1, 2018; April 8, 2018

Meg Jenista Kuykendall—Pastor, The Washington DC Christian Reformed Church,
Washington, DC
October 28, 2018; November 4, 2018; November 11, 2018; November 18, 2018

F. Willis Johnson, Jr.—Pastor, Wellspring Church, Ferguson, MO
December 23, 2018; December 25, 2018; December 30, 2018

John Lee—Pastor, Bethel Christian Reformed Church, Sioux Center, IA
September 30, 2018; October 7, 2018; October 14, 2018; October 21, 2018

Gerald Liu—Assistant Professor of Worship and Preaching, Princeton Theological Seminary, Princeton, NJ
February 25, 2018; March 4, 2018; March 11, 2018; March 18, 2018

DJ del Rosario—Pastor, Bothell United Methodist Church, Bothell, WA
January 6, 2018; January 7, 2018; January 14, 2018; January 21, 2018

Joel Schreurs—Minister of the Word, First Christian Reformed Church, Denver, CO
November 25, 2018; December 2, 2018; December 9, 2018; December 16, 2018

Laura Truax—Pastor, LaSalle Street Church, Chicago, IL
September 2, 2018; September 9, 2018; September 16, 2018; September 23, 2018

Erin Wathen—Pastor, Saint Andrew Christian Church, Olathe, KS
January 28, 2018; February 4, 2018; February 11, 2018; March 25, 2018

Contributors: Full Sermon Texts

O. Wesley Allen, Jr.—Professor of Homiletics, Southern Methodist University, Dallas, TX
"Who Is Calling Whom?" (Mark 10:46-52)

Elisabeth DeVries—Graduate Student in Homiletics, Emmanual College, Toronto, Canada
"Groanings" (Romans 8:18-25)

Scott Hoezee, General Editor—Director, The Center for Excellence in Preaching, Calvin Theological Seminary, Grand Rapids, MI
"The Shrill One" (Luke 3:1-20)

Karoline M. Lewis—Associate Professor of Biblical Preaching, Luther Seminary, Saint Paul, MN
"What Am I Doing Here?" (Mark 1:29-39)

Jacob D. Myers—Assistant Professor of Homiletics, Columbia Theological Seminary, Decatur, GA
"Harmonizing Glory" (Psalm 19)

Luke A. Powery—Associate Professor of Homiletics, Duke Divinity School, Durham, NC
"Why Are You Weeping?" (John 20:1-18)

Subject Index

Index of Scripture